Praise for *In Plain Sight*

"By writing and publishing this book, *In Plain Sight*, Shaun Austin will save veterans' lives. His poetry and reflections on each poem are selfless, insightful, and articulate.

If every veteran, family member and everyone who has ever loved them, who has ever struggled with their mental health, could be as brave and authentic as Shaun in this book, every veteran's world would be a better place. Reading this book will help many of them achieve that. Thank you, Shaun." — Lieutenant General John Caligari AO, DSC (Retired)

"Shaun Austin's poetry is a collection of stories and shared experiences among modern-day soldiers. Shaun uses simple yet profound words that portray thrilling detail into the lives of Veterans from the height of their careers through the darkest of days.

This vulnerability reassures Veterans that you are never really alone." — Casey Nixon, ANZ Veteran Lead Accenture & Veteran Mental Health Ambassador

"Too often, words lose their meaning. Individually they carry definition. Combined with purpose they can be used to inform and inspire, or control and corrupt.

Too often those of us who have served and seen the greatest potential of the human spirit, personified by our ANZACs, often fail to simply communicate and articulate our thoughts and emotions. Because we have not been conditioned to do so, or because we jump to the conclusion that others would not understand.
But through the most simple of expressions, writing these as words on a page, we can often find purpose in their combined meaning, and inspiration right there to last an age."— Heston Russell

"I'm not much of a poet,
Let alone a reader,
The Army chews us up and spits us out a leader,
But I'll never forget my final time walking out that Battalion Gate,
The memory kept alive with a book and a mate.
Shook hands with Sarge
On Route to a medical Discharge
I might be a Lid,
But the love for the boys they'll never get Rid.
Your Book bought that back
That I'm not just a sack"
— Matthew 'Willy' Williams OAM

"Moving, honest and timely, *In Plain Sight* will resonate with anyone who has served, and anyone who has suffered." — Tony Park, veteran and author

IN PLAIN SIGHT

SHAUN AUSTIN

First published in 2022 by BrothersNBooks
Brisbane, QLD, Australia
www.brothersnbooks.com

Publishing services by Noble Books

ISBN 9781761280160

Published in Australia and New Zealand for BrothersNBooks by:

Noble Books, an imprint of Booktopia Group Ltd

Cover art: Ron Bradfield Jnr
In Plain Sight 2020, mixed media, 160 × 65 × 40 cm
Collection of the Australian War Memorial, purchased 2020
Image courtesy of the Australian War Memorial
© Ron Bradfield Jnr

BrothersNBooks is a not-for-profit organisation that establishes community libraries and promotes reading as a form of resilience and growth. The publisher also encourages people to share their own stories of resilience and triumph over adversity on their site www.brothersnbooks.com or simply on their social media pages BrothersNBooks.

Printed and bound in Australia by SOS Print + Media Group

The paper in this book is FSC® certified. FSC® promotes environmentally responsible, socially beneficial and economically viable management of the world's forests.

booktopia.com.au

Disclaimer

Many of the poems and topics in this book can be quite triggering. If you are struggling to get through this book, or if it causes you too much emotional stress, please reach out for help.

If you need immediate support where you are at risk of self-harm, call Lifeline on 13 11 14.

If you are an Australian Defence Force member, veteran, or family of either, you can call Open Arms on 1800 011 046 for access to mental health support.

This book is an expression of my personal experience and is intended for informational purposes only.

Dedication

Our greatest gift is what we give to others.
The chance to give is our gift in return.
We give our all so that others don't suffer.
And for what we've suffered, others shall learn.

Contents

Preface	xiii
Why Poetry?	xvii
The Transition	xix
Why Read?	xxiii
Poetry	xxvii
Brothers	1
Lost at Home	4
Throwing Stones	7
Mutual Support	13
Belong	16
Anger	18
Yarns	20
Poor Man	24
Black Cloud	28
Soliloquy	39
Heart-Stopper	42
Renovate	45
Messy Connections	49

Seven Haiku	53
Lighthouse	59
Tribe	61
Clay	64
Twinkle	70
Galaxies	74
Tall Poppy	80
Heroes	83
Trauma	86
Anxiety	91
Coffee Snobs	99
Bad Investment	101
Suffering	106
Privilege	119
Dawn	122
Birds	126
Dreaming	130
Candle	133
Forgive	138
Meditation	143
Ink	147
After Credits	151

Closing Remarks 157
Acknowledgements 159
References 161

Preface

"Hey boss, got a minute?" One of my soldiers walked into my office.

"Sure, close the door. What's up?"

The soldier sunk into a plastic chair, and despite being a good six and a half feet tall, he may as well have been a small child. Tears welled in his eyes, and he couldn't lift his head. After a minute, the silence broke.

"They're gonna kick me out, aren't they?"

In one moment, I saw a full-grown man, an Australian Army soldier, break down into tears and lose all composure.

I didn't know it then, but that question would resonate deeply for many more of my soldiers confronted by the same fate, and eventually for me as well. I found this so conflicting for all I wanted was to finish my ROSO (my minimum service contract) and be done with it. I was already jaded and looking forward to a life without the outdated rules and excessive control.

Nervously, and aware not to make the situation any more painful for the soldier, I replied, "We haven't received any formal termination notice from your medical review board yet, so I can't say. But I promise to inform you the moment I receive any confirmation."

I knew this was as useful as saying, "Come back tomorrow," but I was at a loss for words. How do you help someone that has been chewed up and broken by the very system designed to train them? His injuries came from physical training, so he didn't feel entitled to medical treatment or to receive any financial support at all. The thought of discharge with full payments for life from DVA was also no consolation, given that the support was not from warlike service and only further invalidated his self-worth.

What started as a lower back injury for this soldier had quickly spiralled into depression.

A few weeks after this conversation came the phone call.

"Hey boss, I'm not ok," he told me. "I don't know what to do. I didn't know who else to call. I need help."

They say the responsibilities of command don't stop when you leave work, but this felt more like responsibility for another human being, for a friend. I drove to his house and took him to a clinic where they could take care of him.

On the drive, he told me about his failed suicide attempt only a week earlier. He took all his meds with a bottle of tequila, and by some miracle, woke up the next morning.

"Thank you for being there," he said. "I just needed someone to listen. No one else cares. My doctor doesn't care. The psych doesn't care. The rehab manager doesn't care. The whole system is fucked."

He paused.

"You're the only person I could tell who would listen."

We talked through it all, and when he was ready to be handed over to their care, I told him I would return the next day to check on him. Finally, I drove home.

I didn't reveal it to him then, but only days earlier, my brother had tried the same thing. He was also in hospital at the same time and under observation for a failed suicide attempt through alcohol and prescription drug overdose. The crazy thing is, when I heard my brother was in hospital, I didn't leave my troop; I had responsibilities to maintain.

For the month or so that the soldier was in hospital I visited him at least once a week, each time asking myself how I could care more about my soldier than my own brother.

Then, when I got back from a visit to the hospital, it all came to a head. My partner asked me to drive her somewhere and as we got into the apartment elevator, I snapped.

"I can't do this anymore!"

Shocked, she responded. "I can take the bus, but that's no reason to get this angry. What's wrong?"

In that moment, she made me realise I couldn't handle the pressure to maintain this façade of normality when I felt I was failing as both a leader and as a brother. I cried right there in the elevator, more than I had ever allowed myself before.

When I sought feedback and support at work, I was told by other officers to not get so emotionally invested. I had 60 soldiers to lead and manage, and if I got this emotional every time someone was depressed, I was headed for a breakdown myself.

Despite this, I maintained close contact with the soldier, and eventually, he was medically separated from the Army. Years later, after another posting and my own experience with being medically discharged, I reached out to him, and it seemed the Army had forgotten about him. When he heard from me, the same words echoed.

"You were the only one who ever cared."

And so, I have written this book for this soldier, and for every soldier who disappeared in plain sight.

Despite all the adversity this soldier faced, he still maintains hope for the future and expresses a genuine concern for others. When we talked, he frequently asked how I was and made sure I had a support network if I was struggling.

This soldier taught me that only someone who had been so thoroughly mistreated by the system could understand the pain enough to reach out and offer support to others in return. He also showed me that we shouldn't need to suffer this process to support each other and we shouldn't wait until we're already out of the military to wrestle with these problems.

It is my hope that this book can help others recognise they're not alone and dispel the shame and stigma to reach out for help.

Why Poetry?

I have chosen poetry as the medium for my expression to share this experience with direct emotion. The poems throughout this book reflect the journey of departing the military and attempting to reintegrate into society, often unsuccessfully.

The cover art and title, *In Plain Sight,* comes from the veteran and artist, Ron Bradfield, Jnr. For me, it highlights how once we leave the military, we feel like we disappear in plain sight. Our pain is hidden, and we may become lost forever.

The shreds of civilian clothing form the ghillie suit which hides the identity of those who can no longer hide behind their uniforms. For some soldiers, life outside the military becomes another form of combat, another world where they must camouflage themselves so others do not see their pain.

It may seem drastic to compare departing from the military with combat, but it's apt if we want to be prepared for it. In the past two decades of conflict in Afghanistan, 41 Australian Defence Force (ADF) members lost their lives on operations. During this same timeframe, according to the Australian Institute for Health and Welfare 1,062 ex-service personnel ended their own lives after departing the military. This data does not include the year

2020, which if estimated from the previous five-year average, would be closer to over 1,130 in total. Whilst I do not wish in any way to disrespect the fallen or the enormity of their sacrifice, it is important to highlight the relative risks soldiers experience after military service.

These figures reveal an uncomfortable truth. In the past 20 years, our people have been over 25 times more likely to die from suicide after departing from the military than from going into combat. This does not include the hundreds of in-service suicides, or the many thousands of veterans struggling with injuries, depression, anxiety, Post Traumatic Stress Disorder (PTSD) or other service-related conditions.

This short book is my attempt to address this tragedy through creative expression, in the hope it may help us all to share our stories, to connect and understand one another in our struggles both during and after service.

The Transition

I joined the military as a way of attaining a university education that my upbringing would never have enabled. As the youngest of seven kids, none of us stayed at home long enough to finish high school.

I started drinking at 12, drugs by 13, at 14 suffered suicidal depression, and by 15, I moved out of home. At 16, I worked 60 hours a week to save enough money, and by 17, I quit drugs and paid my own way back through high school. By 18, I was accepted into the Australian Defence Force Academy (ADFA).

I went from a high school dropout to a mechanical engineer with first-class honours. I thought my hardest struggles were behind me, but after eight years of service, I was medically discharged from the ADF.

On the 11th of Feb 2020, I was a captain in the Australian Army, and by 0730 the next morning, I had boarded a flight to South America with no other plans or direction. I was no one. Despite my upbringing, the sudden and complete loss of identity was the single hardest experience of my life.

Just prior to leaving the Army, I overcame the shame of asking for help and decided to see a professional through Open Arms. There, a psychologist recommended, *The Reality Slap* by Dr Russ Harris, a book that became one of the key reasons I am still here today.

Many other books helped me over the years, so I have placed them in a reference list at the back of this book, as I want to share their lessons with you.

Through this book, I offer readers something personal, and hopefully, relatable. I express the raw emotions and lessons I've learned from these struggles through poetry.

This book aims to break down the barriers to getting help and encourages our veterans to reach out, read books and share their stories. We must remove the stigma from offering and accepting support from each other, and the shame of sharing our stories. Finally, this book is a call to arms to find the *lost veterans* who do not have a support network before they are lost forever.

Whilst this book aims to support our serving members, it is not an administrative guide to transitioning from the military. It is not another resource to understand how to manage medical separation, or how to apply for Department of Veterans Affairs (DVA) support. This type of information is offered by Rehabilitation Managers, the DVA, advocates, and through events such as the transition seminar.

This book does not aim to start another veteran support organisation, as there are many. Instead, I hope it supports existing groups in achieving their mission to reach the people who need it the most.

I was too stubborn to accept all the support that was offered. I attended the transition seminar, thought I didn't need to be there and left early.

Didn't that bite me on the arse...

While there were many veteran groups and associations

available to help me, I didn't engage them. I either wanted to be completely involved in the military, fit and capable to do my job, or I wanted nothing to do with it. My inability to render effective service drove me to avoid anything associated with that life until I finally had to confront it.

I suffered for it, out of pride.

And so, I wrote this book to address a different aspect of the challenge, one that cannot be completed by filling in a form or attending a briefing. I wrote it to address the issue of asking for help. At times, this book is quite raw, and each poem is written as a pure expression of how I felt. It is an expression of my experience; the struggles, and the ways I found to move forward and find meaning. My hope is that by sharing these stories, I may reach you in a time of need.

If you are facing down your transition date, grappling with medical issues or struggling to reintegrate with society, this book is for you.

If you are family or a friend of someone going through this transition, or mental health issues, this book is for you.

If you are battling with mental health issues yourself, be it depression, anxiety or PTSD, this book is for you.

It may just save a life.

Why Read?

Imagine you live in a storage room with only a small amount of light coming through a vent in the wall, which also provides just enough air to breathe. In it is everything you need for subsistence, along with a few books and a TV. You could spend your entire life living in this storeroom binge-watching, eating, drinking, or taking drugs to distract yourself from the claustrophobic existence. Not knowing what's outside, you have no need to look, and the books just look like dusty useless objects: nowhere near as entertaining as what you are watching.

But one day, the TV breaks and keeps playing the same movie on repeat, and you realise you can't turn it off. Now you are more aware than ever of your prison, as the TV reiterates the same negative thoughts — and you can't stop them.

Out of sheer desperation to distract yourself from the TV, you open a book. In it is a key to a door right there in the storage room, one you did not see. You open it.

Once through the door, there is a larger room, with more sunlight and fresh air, and more locked doors. Compelled to find these keys as well, you read the next set of books and find more keys. Each key is a new perspective, and each room a new space to expand your mind.

Now with some distance from the noisy TV, you can cope with its negative *thoughts,* but you still want to fix it.

Eventually, you unlock all the rooms, including to a garage with an entire collection of cars, bikes, boats, and tools. With these new tools, you fix the TV.

Finally, you unlock the front door and walk outside into the beautiful gardens. You realise this entire time, you lived in but a small storeroom within a giant mansion. Now, you have escaped your limited mental construct. You have escaped your mind.

From this vantage point, it doesn't much matter if the TV plays up again, as it is such a small part of your newly found experience. You just allow it to be.

Now imagine after you find this freedom, you go to your neighbour's mansion, and see that he too is living cramped in his limited storeroom, unaware of what he is missing. You talk to him through the vent and say, "There's more to life than this little room. Read books. They will change your life."

Yet he replies, "Nah, I'm good. I've actually got Netflix in here."

"But books will open your eyes!" you say. "They have keys to rooms you don't even know exist."

The purpose of this book, among others, is to give us the keys to our own mental freedom, and eventually, the tools to overcome our challenges. Even if we're not stuck in our heads, a book can offer freedom and even clearer headspace. It can be near impossible to get people to leave the storeroom willingly without them first suffering the prison of their own minds.

Often, intense suffering compels us to seek what lies beyond it, and to search for such keys. Often too, we don't even see that we're in such a small room, if it's all we've ever known. We may even be offended to be told we are living in a storeroom and won't admit our TV is broken or playing negative messages on repeat.

Once we've had enough and wake up to the fact we are in a mental prison, it is hard to stay in there for long. If we don't find a key, we may try a different means of escape, and this is a preventable tragedy. It is important not to hesitate. Once we know we're in a bad headspace, it is critical to find the right keys.

The key could be asking for help from a mate. It could be Open Arms. It could be a book. It could even be our own inner realisation of what we need to do to free ourselves. But if we think the key to getting out of this room is to end it all, why not ask for help first?

We are all afraid of the unknown. Asking for help may open a door to an uncertain room. But if the room we're in now is unbearable, chances are the door leads to a better room; one with a bit more light and fresh air.

I was at the point of opting out of the storeroom when I realised, I could escape it and still keep my life. Now I enjoy the mansion, the cars, the tools, and the gardens and have the chance to help my neighbours.

Had I gone the other way, I would have never known what life could have offered. I would have left believing the world was just a dark and lonely storeroom.

If you feel your life is like this claustrophobic room, reach out for help. Right now. Call a mate.

Call Open Arms. Find anyone and talk. You're not alone in this.

If you aren't convinced to ask for help, at least keep reading this book. We may have more in common than you think. And just maybe, you'll find a key.

Poetry

The following collection of poems is structured as a short story to express my departure from the military, followed by a descent into my own personal hell, and finally, my journey toward purpose and meaning. Some of these poems are simple and direct, expressing the raw emotions of the experience. Others are metaphorical with deeper meaning.

Each poem can be read in isolation, but the collection provides greater insight when read in order. For each poem, allow time to reflect upon it after reading. Consider how it makes you feel and what it says to you, as everyone experiences life differently, even down to the impressions of a single word.

Once you have taken the time to understand whatever comes up for you from reading it, there is a Reflection section to explore the meaning behind it. After reading the Reflection, you're invited to go back and reread the poem to see what feelings it evokes, as it may just allow you to see something you missed.

In some sections, there are deep dives into topics that need more detail. These sections may be confronting but they also provide the most insight and may even contain the keys to overcoming a painful situation.

Once you've read all the poems, find one that resonates the most with you and share it with someone you care about, or someone you think might benefit from it. Sharing new insights is a powerful way to remember them and in turn, to enhance how well we implement them in our own lives.

Finally, I have included a list of resources at the end that have each profoundly changed my life and are well worth the read. They gave me the keys to my freedom.

Brothers

Form up, fall out
Face up, face out
Packs on, darts out
You're up, lead scout

Last act, quick shout
Contact! Wait out
Hats on, ramp down
March on, home bound

PT, mornos
Training, sportos
Repeat, shake out
Refit, post out

Jaded, joint pain
Downgrade, no gain
Rehab, treatment
Relapse, weakness

Broken, feeder
Token, linga
Admin, discharge
Hand in, recharge

Freedom, not so
Boredom, start slow
Purpose, meaning
Service, leaving

Fighting, feeling
Frightening, reeling
Worthless, hopeless
Faceless, pointless

From child, to soldier
From stranger, to brother
Now wild, a loner
From digger, to 'other'

One day, we all leave
And one way, we all grieve
Rejection is quite real
Connection can still heal

So go now, find them
The lost ones, remind them
That always, they're Brothers
In more ways, than others

Brothers – Reflection

The opening poem "Brothers" is an attempt to express the entirety of service in as few words as possible, to highlight that whether you served four years or 40, regardless of corps, role, race, gender or rank, the experience is finite. It ends, one way or another. It is short and sharp to express the harsh reality that for some, it can end as quickly as it started.

The first two lines span from first learning to form up and march, to falling out and graduating training, facing up to reality and responsibility then facing out towards the enemy. In only four lines, someone moves from civilian to soldier.

Likewise, the entire experience of deployment, fear, loss, and returning occurs as a memory that soon passes. It captures the repetitive nature of service and the abrupt end that can come from a service injury.

The decline from purpose in service to worthlessness occurs quickly. For me and many others, it was the defining factor of our struggle with mental health.

This poem is a call to arms for those still serving not to abandon those who have left, no matter the length of their service, for it is a difficult journey that we all must endure.

Lost at Home

In the silence as I pause to reflect
And take stock of my time in service
I ask myself, "Did I have any effect?"
And the uncertainty ahead makes me nervous

Have I made my country proud?
Did I do the Anzac legend justice?
Are my feelings of pain allowed?
Given that I suffered not their injustice

Do we mourn today's unknown soldier?
Whose body we can't repatriate
Lost at home from the burden they shoulder
The casualties of a system we create

How many more shall grow not old?
As we that are left say with regret
The solemn oath that we've been told
To those forgotten "Lest we forget"

Lost at Home – Reflection

"Lost at Home" summarises the journey and the challenge we face to come to terms with our service ending. While we uphold ourselves to the highest ideals—the Anzac legend—we remember their sacrifice but undervalue our own.

The ending of our service represents our last chance to accomplish whatever it is we set out to do, which is an ever-shifting target. Many of us leave, having felt a missed opportunity, and that we didn't give enough. Perhaps some of us experience survivor guilt, that we made it through, but our mates didn't. This is a quality of pain we may not feel we deserve to express. Perhaps we feel our pain is nothing compared to the sacrifice of the fallen, or that of the Anzacs, but by trivialising our pain, we hide it and it festers.

Which is worse: a broken bone that gets mended with rehab or a fracture that isn't set and we pretend doesn't exist?

Many of us live with these constant yet invisible aches: loss, grief, guilt, shame, or repressed anger. Whether or not we feel allowed to have this pain, if we do, it is better to acknowledge it and heal, then to let it eat away at us until we snap. Some of us will hide it until we have an outburst and hurt the people we love, while others will hide it until we hurt ourselves.

The unknown soldier is the symbol of those lost overseas without the chance for repatriation or named burial. The group of unknown soldiers I refer to here are the veterans who vanish into society once they leave the military, broken and without identity, and who end their lives unable to express this pain. This book is dedicated to them and is written in the hopes of reaching the next generation in time to heal these fractures.

Throwing Stones

They said "words mean things"
A very insightful lesson
Though the instructors were rarely "Pacific"
It was more important the vowels were on point

"Elf, height, elf, hi, elf, I, elf!"
Dulcet tones of a dargin's call
Nothing sweeter than the parrot's morning chirp
"Reveille! Reveille! Reveille!"

"Hurry up, don't run!" after all
Slow is smooth, smooth is fast
Though the smoothest always came in last
As the shouts echoed through the valley

I was amazed how though I grew up
Around farms and firearms
The marksmanship coaches only made me miss
Who'd have thought yelling would piss off the firers

"We're not here to fuck spiders!"
Well then, I have no idea why I'm here
My rifle is cleaner than my brew mug could dream
And I'm out of stones to throw at the shed

Can't even call it a bed
Cause now it's "me-farter"
Thanks to the hotbox mystery meats
And the fragrant hint of dank socks

"I think I need to recalibrate"
As the knife hand points
What's the effective range of a blank stare?
As they zero in on the poor bastard taking hits

The Steyr sits snug to my side
As I hide the hangover with false pride
Staving off the collapse as a hero
Doesn't take a knee on parade

Crash, there goes someone's teeth
More casualties than by the butter knife
In the sheath, a bayonet for the course
of plastic targets and adrenaline

Then again, I must admit
I lived for those adrenal hits
The morbid curiosity that makes you
Sniff the CS gas just a bit

I loved using Vietnam era webbing,
And CBRN gear
that seemed like it would only increase
the risk of exposure

Glad that it's over, you peel off the sweatsuit
The rubber boots and gloves
And shove the mask in your Have-a-Sack
Some false security for the next attack

Thank goodness for TBAS and SCE
So we could tie the quick release tabs
To the DP1 cage and watch someone rage
As it falls apart in their hands

Grandstand position made it easy
to see the PTIs explain the days pain
I thought they were called lobsters for the red shorts
Some say it meant body full of muscle, head full of shit

Say what you want, they made us all fit
We learnt not to quit, and to help out the weak
And seek teamwork over individual success
That the ticket to freedom is discipline

Though all I wished on those endless piquets
Was to escape
I kind of miss the mindless shit talk
And the landscape of a stand-to sunrise

To my surprise I still cringe
When my mates that are in the green
Talk of pointless courses and shit postings
Of missed deployments they were once boasting

I want the Army to change
So those that remain get a better run
Though the rising sun is a powerful symbol
There are many jaded who would leave it behind

Blind, I was one of them
Yet it means more to me now than ever
And I can't sever the ties
Or let the memories fade

I'm just glad to have played the game
And if it's all the same
The training was worth it to look back and know
Everything will be ok, I've been through worse

Though I never got the chance
To put this training to the test
The best I knew that did
Seemed to agree it prepared them well

Somewhere between the drill and field
The skills were sealed in these members
Who served with mates they could trust
Would bust their back for each other

Maybe what I remember is
The bullshit that built camaraderie
It's hard to see but part of me
Grew stronger through the misery

When all you can do is laugh or you'll cry
You try to see the humour
And half the value of training comes
In learning to laugh at the absurd

Throwing Stones – Reflection

"Throwing Stones" is a free-flowing expression of the feelings, thoughts, and memories tied together with the sense that what was most absurd about our training is what made it so valuable.

It took me a long time to look back fondly on my experience in the Army, and I went through quite a dark time until I could appreciate everything I had in life, including the things that seemed ridiculous at the time.

Mutual Support

I have overcome my physical injury and the pain
But it seems my journey is far from over
More difficult to come is the mental strain
Which my dreams remind me moreover

I could deal with a pack, gat, armour and heat
And together we conquered all hardship
Yet alone I feel my mind heavy on my feet
And they drag on the ground through this hard shit

"Speak up!", "Reach out!", "Why won't you talk?"
Surrounded by options but silenced by pride
It's when we most need help that alone we walk
And try to take it all in our stride

We must both engage for it to be mutual support
Otherwise, you are just taking out the enemy for me
While I sit with my gun jammed and report
That everything's fine, just ignore me

Perhaps my self-loathing will give way to love one day
And I'll remember what it feels like to be human
Until then my clothing will give me reason to stay
As another member of this ill-defined movement

Mutual Support – Reflection

I wrote "Mutual Support" while frustrated with myself for being unwilling to accept help. Although I needed support, I was too stubborn, too proud, and maybe too independent to accept it.

We all need to feel that we're capable of handling whatever life throws at us. A sense of control is key to managing uncertainty, fear, pain and chaos. When we feel we have no control in facing a situation, we can feel overwhelmed, even when someone else offers to help.

Mutual support is when two weapon systems cover each other's arcs or fields of fire. If two guns cover one side of a hill, it is difficult for the enemy to overrun our position. Even when one gun is reloading, the other can cover it.

If our gun is jammed, and we can't support the other gun, they are now taking out the enemy alone and we risk being overrun, so it is critical to communicate as soon as we have a problem so they can support us until we're back up and running. Even if the other gun can take out the enemy alone, we may feel pretty worthless if we aren't doing our part.

In the same way, despite many people offering me mutual support to take out my own internal enemy, I felt worthless that I couldn't take it out on my own. But we would almost never be placed alone on a hill, and further, if we're covering a mate whose gun has jammed, would we want them to keep quiet or tell us there's a problem?

Now when I feel hesitant to ask for help, I consider what I'd want a mate to do, and I'd want them to ask me. I'd never wish for a mate to suffer alone, so why should I tell myself to do that?

Finally, the "clothing" of the "ill-defined movement" is the group of veterans who become invisible once they're in civilian clothing, and yet they are all part of a movement. In the beginning, I felt self-loathing by being a part of this invisible group, but now it's the source of my strength.

All veterans, no matter the length of their service, share a connection. We are all part of something greater.

Belong

I dream my deepest memories are lies
That my past didn't happen
I disguise my service in long hair and a pen
I despise myself for feeling

Reminiscing I forget, what I remember
Doesn't fit within my identity
Like reflections in the mud, I distort
And my mind can't settle on truth

They all keep going forward, I alone wander
Aimlessly, I wonder the meaning I alone can answer
Stronger than the urge to rest is to belong
The rest grow stronger together, while I long

Belong – Reflection

"Belong" is a reflection on the recurring dreams I had after leaving the Army. In many ways, I felt as though I had never served, and never completed what I set out to do. It is like my mind wanted to forget about the military as it hurt too much to consider that all my mates were continuing without me.

The need to disguise myself comes from the feeling that I am not a "real" veteran. I don't have injuries from warlike service or PTSD, and though I served eight years, I don't feel I deserve the support of others. This view stopped me from seeking help for a long time and in the end, only deepened my suffering.

Regardless of how long we serve, it changes us. We are a part of something with unique challenges that don't end once we hand back the uniform. Anyone who has served deserves support.

Consider it this way: we have volunteered a period of our lives that we will never get back, to serve others before ourselves. Whether or not we have deployed, if we have served, we are veterans.

Anger

Anger overpowers
Anger consumes
The rage it builds
Shattering all ideals

Pouring down
Like a rapid
Flowing through
All I have left

In its wake
Is a vacuous mess
An empty guilt
And a broken heart

I am shattered
By what I most need
To heal this pain
And let love in

Anger – Reflection

I wrote "Anger" after an intense rage at myself and those around me. While I have never been one for physical violence or outbursts of anger, the feeling consumes me from within when I don't confront it or let it out, so I shut down instead.

I was angry at myself for wanting to leave the Army, then I was angry at myself for wanting to go back. I was angry at those who had taken me in, and angry at the same people for having expectations of me to get back to my own life. I was angry at my partner for not understanding what I was going through, and angry when she did understand and tried to help. I was angry because I was vulnerable, and it was my last defence from being exposed.

The line "I am shattered by what I most need" expresses the frustration of needing and wanting support, yet constantly pushing it away out of a fear of vulnerability.

The later poem, "Renovate", explores this idea along with other issues of emotional expression and healing.

Yarns

There were shreds and threads of a self
Entangled like a ghillie suit to hide
In plain sight the many identities
It is always easier to tie knots than to untangle

This patchwork now a ball of yarn
Holds all the yarns and spin
And where to begin to pick apart
The stitches that conceal my heart

I don't want to lose the threads that link
My new self to this great web of meaning
But now I trip on these very strings
And like a poorly set perimeter cord I walk in circles

They are the greatest forces in our nature
To belong and yet to expand
To join in song or to disband
This conflict is the only constant as we mature

For however much I yearned to escape
Freedom is more like drifting at sea
Perhaps the key to uplifting service is this
To spread our wings yet fly together

Yarns – Reflection

"Yarns" was inspired by a visit to the Australian War Memorial, a few months after I discharged. It is named after the winner of the 2020 Napier Waller Art Prize. The winning piece titled *Yarn* by Matt Jones, was a signal flag made of yarns, tied together to form the Navy Kilo sign which means "I want to communicate with you".

It hit me so powerfully as both a call for help and to connect that I started to tear up. The collective hit of all the art on display pulled at all the loose stings holding me together and confronted the emotions I'd tried to bury. This poem is a reflection of those conflicting feelings.

The "shreds and threads of a self" refers to the artwork by Ron Bradfield Jnr titled *In Plain Sight*—the cover art of this book, which is a ghillie suit made of torn up bright t-shirts that the ex-sailor used to cover up his identity as an Indigenous man. After leaving the Navy, he felt, once again, judged for his race rather than accepted for his rank and uniform.

For me, this resonated with the feeling that once I took off my army uniform for the final time, I went back in time to the identity I had before I joined. It felt like I had returned to be the troubled coastal kid with depression and drug and alcohol problems. I felt the need to hide my identity as a former military member, so I grew long hair and a goatee and wore the same set of old clothes for months on end. I didn't know who I was anymore, or who I wanted to be.

Through this poem I tried to express the conflicting feelings of wanting to be part of the military and yet, at the same time, wanting to put it all behind me. It is the desire to be free and yet to belong.

The statement "It is always easier to tie knots than to untangle" can be applied to everything in life, from relationships and military service to earphones and perimeter cord. The perimeter cord, that thin, green cord we tie around the trees to signify the boundary of our position, grows into a metaphor in this poem. At night, it serves as a guide to stay on the walking tracks and not get lost moving around a position. A large circle of cords merge with each person's position. If the cord is tied wrong, it can be hard to find our mates in the dark. Every time we change positions, we pack up this cord and if we do it poorly, it is a tangled mess.

My desire to put the military behind me—to change my position—tangled all these cords so I could no longer find and connect with my mates. For another example, earphones in our pocket, grow tangled over time. So too when we put people into the military, they become tangled over time, across identities and their relationships.

Unfortunately, when we take earphones out of our pocket, time doesn't magically untangle them. We have to sort out the mess patiently. Departing the military leaves us with tangled connections that won't magically sort themselves out either. It takes work.

The final lines and the "key to uplifting service" calls

us to balance the need for individual freedom, purpose and initiative, with a collective mission and vision. We all want freedom and control over our lives, but we still want to be part of a team. Allowing people to follow their own purpose and passions—be it fitness, education, sport, music, business, family or volunteering—we can get the best from our teams while maintaining a collective purpose.

I had soldiers who balanced their work while winning world championships in body building. Others completed engineering degrees while working as craftsmen. I had peers who volunteered for the Red Cross or worked with the United Nations outside of the military when on long service leave. Many others simply did their best to be with their families whenever they could.

We each have our own drive to serve and yet be free to follow our passion, and the best soldiers and officers I had the chance to serve with did both. Their freedom allowed them to fly high and set the example, while still flying together.

Poor Man

Poor man,
what little you know in your wisdom.
Your trials fail in comparison
to the immensity of your self-burden.
You fall at the site of uncertainty,
a calamity in your eyes.
But lies they are to free yourself,
from the reality of your dismal attempts to better it.
You stormed the pit of sorrow
only to be impaled on your own bayonet.
Yet, you cry at the enemy, they are to blame.
But shame on you and your self-pity.
Disgusted you should be.
For you are free to revel in this day,
far away from the true hurt hearts.
That start and stop in a withered body,
stray from such concepts of health.
Where wealth is measured in water,
that runs dry before your tears.
Where fears keep blood pumping
faster than any gears
keep your malicious melancholy machine
on the deadline to your next pay check
You're a wreck of greed and ignorance,
the pinnacle of human achievement.
A statement to the designer that we are done.

Poor Man – Reflection

I wrote "Poor Man" from a deep state of depression. It was an outpouring of my own inner critic, so ashamed of myself for struggling when there are clearly people out there worse off than me. It's easy to criticise ourselves and feel ashamed if we haven't met our own expectations. It's easy to feel "not good enough".

In my first year in the Army, my supervising officer said, "Not good enough!" every time we did something wrong. I was left wondering, what is good enough? It is very subjective because it is always possible to do better.

I was achieving high distinctions in my university studies; my fitness was continually improving; I was saving money, engaging in hobbies, and spending time with good mates. Yet somehow, I was still, "not good enough".

Those words burnt into me as my quick response to failure.

Not "I'll do better next time".

Not "Everyone makes mistakes".

Not "I did my best, but I will strive to be better".

Simply "Not good enough!"

The book *The Reality Slap* refers to these "Not Good Enough" moments as NGEs and offers strategies to manage them, which I integrated into the later poems "Anxiety" and "Meditation".

I have always struggled with the inner critic and the anxiety it creates, but I kept it at bay by pushing my own limits. When told I was a failure and shouldn't go back to high school, I ranked in the top 5% of the state, and second in my school. When I was told by that officer that no one gets high distinctions in university in all of their subjects, I proved her wrong. When I was told I would be a bad leader, I commanded a troop of 60 soldiers and ranked as the top performing lieutenant out of the 14 in my regiment. When I was diagnosed with lumbar spondylosis and told I couldn't carry a pack or run anymore, I completed the 96km Kokoda challenge with a team of my soldiers just to push this limit.

I don't say all this to "toot my own horn", as these examples were unhealthy in many ways. Although some of my hard work was driven by purpose and a belief in myself, many of my successes were fuelled by a fear of failure or by not being good enough.

This strategy caught up with me once I left the Army, for how could I outshine myself now? How could I silence the NGEs? If I couldn't keep pushing my own limits, I would have to confront this critic, and learn to accept myself.

Being medically discharged was something that I pushed for as I didn't see myself rendering effective service when I couldn't deploy, couldn't eat ration packs, and couldn't go on field exercises. Although I saw it coming, it still destroyed all my successes in one shattering blow.

I was no longer the captain who promoted six months ahead of his peers; the high performing, hardworking, and contributing member of the Army. I was no one. I was less than no one: I was broken; I was a failure; I was deemed unfit for service; I was by all means "not good enough" by my own standards and the Army's.

In my state of depression, I felt unworthy of even feeling sadness. In my mind, there were starving people living in poverty or war who truly had reason to suffer. Not me.

It took me a long time to reach this point, but I finally came to understand that pain and suffering are relative. Although we may say that others are objectively suffering more than we are, it doesn't help us overcome the suffering. Viktor Frankl, a holocaust survivor and psychiatrist, highlights this relationship with suffering in his great book *Man's Search for Meaning.*

"To draw an analogy: a man's suffering is similar to the behavior of a gas. If a certain quantity of gas is pumped into an empty chamber, it will fill the chamber completely and evenly, no matter how big the chamber. Thus suffering completely fills the human soul and conscious mind, no matter whether the suffering is great or little. Therefore the 'size' of human suffering is absolutely relative."

We must first accept that the NGE isn't helping us. It isn't going to make us better in the long term.

Once we accept this, we must accept that it is ok to feel pain and emotions.

Finally, we must accept ourselves, as we are.

Black Cloud

I wake up to a feeling of dread
Empty yet heavy, heart pounding, yet dead
There is a brief euphoria as I draw breath
Then the inevitable collapse as I exhale death

Like a hot night with one leg under the sheet
I lay half in life, unable, incomplete
The clear horizon between ocean and sky
Now a fog that blurs what it is to die

When your every identity has faded to grey
And your sense of belonging has turned you away
You begin to question your very existence
And doubt that your mind has any real substance

It is from this state that I stare to the abyss
And look back to you all, and think "What did I miss?"
For it seems there's no meaning to why I am here
So without any purpose it's goodbye I fear

There are many ways I have thought to go
The bottle, meds, or just veer off the road
It just seems insane that I'd prefer nothing
Than continue a life that makes me feel something

But this is the problem that others don't see
I'm stuck in a black cloud, I cannot break free
So rather would I face the end
Than poison the world, my family and friends

They've suffered enough, and so have I
But now I can't keep up this lie
I know it's selfish to leave like this
But I have no option, "What one did I miss?"

My final chance was to be heard
But to reach for help would be absurd
Surely if I'm about to go
How bad can it be for my pain to show?

I asked for help without real hope
I didn't think it would stop the rope
But I broke down in tears and lost control
And soon my mates had saved my soul

The black cloud lifted enough to find
I wasn't alone inside my mind
Others have these thoughts as well
And there are ways to escape this hell

I started small and shared my story
It wasn't much, no courageous warry
But the cloud kept clearing till I saw the light
Now I have the strength to continue the fight

There's power in vulnerability
So fuck off pride and dignity
What had I missed to keep on living?
To support each other and keep on giving

Black Cloud – Reflection

Through "Black Cloud", I wanted to express what it feels like to be suicidal, to be misunderstood and to not want help. I wanted to share this so people encountering this intense state wouldn't feel alone and could see that there is hope in asking for help. Further, I hoped those on the outside could see a glimpse from within, so they may understand better to be able to help.

I have shared my story below in more detail as an example of what it is like to go through this experience. This section may be confronting; however, it also holds the key for those struggling with this issue.

I hope this story helps you to relate to the truth behind the statement "there's power in vulnerability". If you are in the Black Cloud, you are not alone, and there is a better way out. Ask for help.

And if you are not in this dark place, I hope it helps you reach someone else who is.

Asking for Help

Leaving the Army was not the first time I faced suicidal depression. As a teenager, I was suicidal for many reasons and left home at 15 to escape from a bad situation. I numbed myself with drugs and work to cope with the emotions, without learning to deal with them. When I quit drugs and paid my way back through high school, I developed a sense of purpose and belief that drove me to overcome my fears and obstacles. I believed I could be better and didn't have to settle for any situation. I found purpose in using my experience to help others.

At 27, I found myself confronted by the same struggle with suicide when I once again lost purpose and belief in myself. My medical discharge from the Army resulted from a condition which, to me, was embarrassing. I was diagnosed with coeliac disease. Although it is an autoimmune condition that carries with it other increased risks like cancer, I was effectively being discharged because I couldn't eat bread. I felt completely invalidated as a contributing member of the team. I could no longer attend training exercises due to my adverse reactions to both the ration packs and the mess food.

Over the six months that followed the diagnosis, I lost 10kg and continued to struggle with malnourishment due to the damage to my gut lining. When the gastroenterologist stated, "This is the worst case I've seen in my 25 years of practice," I knew I wasn't going to be able to continue my service much longer.

Prior to this diagnosis, I had developed three bulged discs and a tear in my lumbar spine that were progressively getting worse. At one point, I could no longer pack march, run, or drive without extreme pain. I sold my manual car for an auto as using the clutch sent my back into spasm and I could no longer conduct PT to the same level with the team.

After many physiotherapists, exercise physiologists and other specialists and scans, I met with an orthopaedic surgeon who told me, "The only way to fix this and stop the pain is to undergo spinal surgery to fuse the vertebrae." He then said this surgery wasn't recommended for anyone under 75 due to its low success rate and frequency of follow-on surgeries.

I felt broken, useless, trapped and a failure. I didn't want to believe the diagnosis, so I continued with my own training and research, but every time I experienced progress, I relapsed.

After 12 months of a strict diet and training, the visit to the gastroenterologist revealed that my condition hadn't improved, with severe damage still visible to my gut lining.

I started to lose faith in the medical system and sought external support for the back issues through a chiropractor and osteopath, but both just cost me thousands of dollars with no results. It was at this point that I decided to face the growing anxiety and depression by seeing a psychologist.

My partner and I were long distance at the time, and

when I told her that I wanted to see a psychologist, it didn't go well at first. I hadn't revealed to her how bad I had been doing, so to her, it just seemed like a breach of trust and intimacy to ask someone else for help. Surely, I could talk to her about anything in my life, but I wasn't ready to open up to her about all of this. Soon enough, she apologised and supported my need to get professional help.

In hindsight, I understand her resistance. It is understandable for others to feel that seeing a psychologist is a breach of trust or intimacy, but a professional can help us in ways a partner or family cannot.

For partners or family members, support is critical. Shaming loved ones for seeking help can be very damaging and dangerous. In time, they may be able to open up to you, but a psychologist can help get them to that point of openness.

Once I had my partner's support, it was far easier going to see a psychologist and to release the shame around it.

Unfortunately, the first psychologist I visited spent six months comforting me, with no strategies to get better, deepening my feelings of worthlessness. With no improvement in my health and no other treatments to try, I felt like I had completely run out of options and hope.

It was then that the Black Cloud consumed me and I didn't want to live anymore. Between my illness, injury, pain and shame, I was broken. I was no longer part of the team, no longer capable, not good enough. I was weak.

I remember walking to a mate's apartment for a rooftop party with a six-pack of gluten-free beers in hand thinking about just jumping off the roof when no one was looking.

Just as the thought came to mind, a beer slipped out of the box and shattered on the road. It instantly woke me up from my depressive state. As I cleaned the broken glass off the road, I considered how I cared so much about cleaning the glass for others and yet I would jump from the top of that building shattering not just my body, but the lives of those who cared about me. I had thought of many more inconspicuous ways of ending it, but that moment made me see the effects of my thinking.

I called my partner and poured out my heart: all the pain and hopelessness and she listened. She talked to my friends and soon they were also calling me to talk and although nothing had changed, everything had changed.

The weight of suicide is heaviest when it's kept inside, and the moment I spoke out it became an easier burden to shoulder. Once my partner understood the depth of my pain, she worked miracles to keep me supported. She quit her job overseas to move back with me. She learned techniques to help me when I struggled with anxiety and gave me the love I needed to heal. It was this small lifting of the clouds that gave me the hope to try again with a second psychologist.

Within the first session, the new psychologist restored my hope. She opened my eyes to my problems and gave me tools to deal with them. Two sessions later, she had me confident to make the transition from the Army and confront my depression and anxiety.

At this point, I thought my problems were again behind me, however, this was only the beginning of the journey. Despite all the suffering, frustration, and pain, none of it compared to the feelings of emptiness and purposelessness that consumed me in the months after leaving the Army.

At first it was a holiday. I could relax, eat healthy, and completely control my activities and exercise. I could do everything at my own pace. The stress melted away, the back pain became more manageable, and my health improved. But after two months of no direction, I began to lose my sense of identity, belonging, values and purpose. The black cloud returned. I went from being deeply connected to something bigger than myself to invisible. I tried to apply all the techniques that my psychologist had taught me, but I continued to spiral downwards without a sense of purpose or belief in myself.

Knowing the power of vulnerability, I talked openly with my partner, family and close friends about how I was feeling. Each of them helped clear the black cloud enough for me to find my purpose in helping others and the belief that my situation would improve.

For me, this feeling was not a demon I could kill that would go away forever. Instead, I've learned to face it head on every time it rears its ugly head. It was when I ignored the demon or refused to talk about it that it grew in the shadows and pulled me down. Armed with early warning signs for when anxiety, depression or suicidal thoughts are building, I know how to deal with them and when to ask for help. Some of the later poems and their reflections, mainly "Meditation" and "Anxiety" cover these methods and approaches.

If you are struggling and don't know who to turn to, please call Lifeline on 13 11 14 and ask for help.

If you are a military member or family member struggling with any mental health issues, don't hesitate to call Open Arms on 1800 011 046. They saved my life, and they may just save yours.

Finally, if you do not want to reach out to these organisations, reach out to someone, anyone, for they will be more willing to help than you may think.

If you are not struggling with these issues or have overcome them yourself, consider how you might help someone else.

Soliloquy

Spilling a soliloquy invisibly
I waste away the words to mask the misery
Voiceless ventriloquy avoiding vanity
The paper forms the freedom for my sanity

Written where the ink can find expression
I pay no mind to if it finds a deep impression
Anxiety and depression overcome with all the lessons
Yet I lose them all to time or to repression

Countless words I found absurd, allowed to vanish
All the notebooks filled with poetry I banish
Fear of failure or judgement and scrutiny
I throw away my thoughts into obscurity

Only now can I see a higher purpose
These words and what they say were never worthless
If I offer them in service, there's more than on the surface
I can use my pain as fuel to make this worth it

Soliloquy – Reflection

"Soliloquy" describes how the process of writing poetry helped me find my purpose and freed me from negative emotions and experiences. A soliloquy is a stream of thought spoken by an actor in a play either alone on stage or in a way not heard by other characters.

For me, "spilling a soliloquy invisibly" was the process of writing poetry to express my feelings, then throwing them away. I don't know how many poems I lost in this process, but it was in sharing them with friends who were struggling that I found meaning in keeping them.

If we don't grow from our experiences and cannot understand them, they consume us. By finding meaning in our suffering, we can use it as fuel to help others enduring the same struggles. Art, music, and any other creative medium give us ways to relate our experiences when we otherwise struggle to find expression, just like the Napier Waller Art Prize that was mentioned in "Yarns".

No matter how talented we may feel, when we try drawing as a way of expressing what is hidden within us, we may be surprised how much it can help. If we don't want to draw, we can write. Write anything. It doesn't have to make sense; it just has to be released.

We can also consider integrating our emotions into exercise. For repressed anger, we can fuel our training with it. For deep sadness, we can demonstrate to ourselves that we are strong enough to overcome it. If we can no longer train due to injury or illness, we can release it when we yell, sing, cry or laugh. It's incredible how much we store that never gets expressed because we aren't conscious of it. It may stay hidden for years until we give it a medium to be released.

Take the time now to find a medium, any medium, and release whatever comes to mind.

Heart-Stopper

I take a dash of the ratpack hot chocolate
And a splash of the Jetboil water
Two sachets of coffee in my pocket
And the remaining condensed milk and sugar

With the lid on my LifeVenture thermos
And a good shake or two for a mixer
Get ready for the coming heart murmurs
When you sip on this pure elixir

If your hands weren't already shaking
From the cold of your 2AM piquet
Then this concoction of caffeine I'm making
Will ensure that you're numb when you lick it

Two sips of this lifesaving brew
Will keep you awake good and proper
Drink it all and you'll see why it's true
That it came to be called the "heart-stopper"

Heart-Stopper – Reflection

I couldn't write a book without mentioning coffee. I used to have the nickname "Brew Wizard", because no matter the time of day or night, or how long we'd been out bush without stopping, I always had a fresh brew to share.

The heart-stopper was a reliable source of energy when morale was low. Sometimes it was thicker than the instant mash and we just about had to chew it.

It seems to be the stupid things that I remember most. Trading ratpack meals, "rats", sleeping in the back of armoured vehicles, having our weapons inspected by someone with tiny hands and dreading what they'll find, or that horrible feeling when someone whispers in our ears "You're on piquet".

I lived brew to brew, with long bouts of ridiculous activities in between. What I've really come to appreciate is that what made those brews special was the people who shared them with me. Those brief moments of respite between intense training or long monotonous periods of boredom made everything more bearable.

I don't feel like my life has as many ridiculous challenges since leaving the Army, or at least, the challenges now are more often faced alone. I miss the collective suffering because when we shared in the pain, it intensified the celebrations at the end.

Perhaps the key is to find something worth suffering for, and to find others willing to struggle for that purpose too, so when the day is done, you can share a beer or a brew, knowing you got through it together.

Renovate

Love is often overlooked in the myriad of tools
The box is filled with many emotions, many misused by fools
A father's gift to any son is to teach each by their use
And never to use anger to achieve as an excuse

For life is full of building, of crafting and of skill
At some points renovation to renew what times made ill
And each of life's great problems can be fixed from your toolbelt
A craftsman keeps them clean and sharp for whatever hand is dealt

Never use an axe when a well-placed chisel will spare
Shattering the life you've built and turning to despair
But if you use a hammer to embed a bloody screw
You'll end up sending splinters into everything you do

Many do not know this, many have not been taught
Their parents lacked the skilful use to pass on what they thought
Instead, there's many lumberjacks who mimicked what they saw
Their parents quick to wield an axe, turning anger into war

Armed with only weapons, it's no wonder they get hurt
They try to build connection, but for this you can't assert
The first step is reflection, to see what needs to change
An honest look, in every crook, a thorough rearrange

Your life so far is a house and yard your parents helped create
But now the work is squarely yours to start to renovate
Once we see the problems and begin to understand
We get to know the tools we need, the ones to keep on hand

Look beyond the picket fence, the paint and well mowed lawn
There are termites in the woodwork, the basement lights are gone
The floorboards creek, the roof still leaks, the carpet has a smell
The plants have died, the weeds all thrive, the garage door is hell

It's not to be a pessimist to focus on the flaws
But awareness leads to action when we've sharpened all our saws
Knowing now the work ahead, you need no trip to bunnings
The tools are all inside your head and books will keep them running

Renovate – Reflection

"Renovate" is another metaphor for how we view our problems and the ways to fix them. We can try our best to be perfect in the eyes of others, with well mowed lawns and painted fences, but we know deep down there are things we hide from others that we need to mend. I excelled in academics and military training. I was clean-cut with a well-ironed uniform and straight arms on the march, but it just hid the festering wounds underneath.

Stripped bare of the dress and bearing, I was frail. The work I needed to do required different tools from stoic discipline. It required self-compassion, acceptance, forgiveness, and authenticity—all easier said than done.

If your parents taught you how to use these tools, it is far more likely you could be resilient in the face of the difficulties of military service. But ironically, people who come from broken homes, where they were taught to choose the axe over the chisel, are more likely to join the military and are the least emotionally prepared for its challenges.

It would seem to be more logical that people who experienced childhood trauma would have better coping strategies for later trauma in life, but often, the opposite is true. For me, the coping mechanisms I found in childhood were either to shut down, focus on tasks or problem-solving, to take the blame for everything, to try please other people, or to be perfect to avoid conflict. Some of these tools were useful for the military. Perfectionism reinforces attention to detail. Problem solving whilst ignoring our inner emotional state is key to mission planning and execution. The stoic minded can overcome pain, but these can be the very people who hide behind a painted fence until the house collapses from termites eating away from the inside. And none of these coping strategies were useful in helping me truly deal with longer term pain or trauma.

As the poem states at the end, it is not through a pessimistic outlook, but the realistic appreciation of the renovation required that shows us the right tools to fix it.

Messy Connections

You are about to embark on a journey
A journey of courage and sacrifice
Where strength will not suffice
To survive the fight

The right attitude is key to success
And the rest of your time after service
Will be marked by these connections
The mateship beyond your mission

Once you leave these gates
Your fates will be forever linked
A bond that breaks only
When you choose to stop believing in it

Outside there will be no more deployments
No more postings to reunite
Or courses to reconnect
No more meals at the mess with old mates

You may take it for granted
To be planted in places with these
Familiar faces of friends long forgotten
You've gotten a gift many don't receive

So when you leave understand this
These connections are in your hands
Don't wait for those coincidental catch-ups
Those serendipitous sightings

There are no more mess games
Compulsory fun boozer parades
Dining-in nights or regiment balls
Only the calls you choose to make

Don't lose these connections
Waiting for some opportunity to arise
Embrace any chance to enhance them
For depression is just loneliness in disguise

Messy Connections – Reflection

"Messy Connections" is a reflection on the book *Lost Connections* by Johann Hari. A friend of mine recommended it to me and it gave me so much perspective. It showed me that my depression was the loneliness from lost and messy connections. The tangled strings from "Yarns" covers the same theme: we need to work actively to maintain these connections once we leave the military.

The line "depression is just loneliness in disguise", refers to how we see depression sometimes as a disease or condition independent of our environment or situation. In reality, depression is largely caused by our relationship to others and the world around us. It is a response to our loneliness and our disconnection from our identity, values, meaning and from nature.

If you have been diagnosed with depression, anxiety, or another condition in which you have been prescribed antidepressants or other mood-altering medications, please read Johann Hari's book. The insight into the over-prescription of these medications provides evidence-based alternatives of how to treat depression and anxiety, so that we don't need to rely on a substance for the rest of our lives. The work also highlights the deep flaws in our individualist world view, and how in many cases, our culture is the cause of the global increase in depression and anxiety.

Lost Connections served as inspiration for the following set of poems "Seven Haiku", which cover what I believe are the main causes of depression and anxiety. These seven poems are only three lines each, to condense what this book has to offer into as few pages as possible.

Seven Haiku

Loneliness

Independently
We struggle to bear a load
Designed to be shared

Disconnection from Nature

Infinite ego
Expand in boundless nature
Insignificant

Meaningless Work

Working to survive
Slavery with extra steps
Live to contribute

Insecure Status

Hierarchical life
The illusion of climbing
But never enough

Poor Values

Pleasure now prevails
Forever yearning for more
When truth satisfies

Childhood Trauma

Personality
Past portrayed as the present
To be overcome

No Hope for the Future

Future vanishes
Fear and pain have paused the clock
Hope restores time

Seven Haiku – Reflection

The "Seven Haiku" each address a different cause of depression as I understand it. The book *Lost Connections* lists nine causes of depression, but I have left out biology and genetics. While these are contributing factors to depression, they're not necessarily causes we can immediately change. Our biology and genetics respond to our environment, so if we want to work on these, we must change our environment.

The seven causes that we can work on directly are explored in this set of poems. These are loneliness or loss of connection to others, disconnection from nature, disconnection from meaningful work, insecurity from status, poor values, childhood trauma, and loss of hope for the future. Whilst this book is primarily a reflection of my personal experience, I reference the seven causes from *Lost Connections* as the most useful tools I found in overcoming depression and anxiety.

When I read *Lost Connections*, I experienced an Aha! moment like the mansion all over again. This book outlined what was wrong in my life and how to fix it. It gave me a sense of understanding and control that allowed me to move forward tangibly, beyond just a bunch of coping strategies.

If I am feeling anxious, it is very important to have the tools to calm myself down, but it is even more effective if I address the source of my anxiety in the first place. With depression as well, I can go out and do something to make myself happy, but the depression will just return unless

I address the causes. This may sound very simple, but it's easy to avoid the root cause of our problems. Many of us mask our emotional discomfort with temporary solutions.

Feeling lonely? Go on social media or be around more people.

Feeling depressed? Watch Netflix or drink.

Feeling disconnected from your work? Complain about it.

Feeling disconnected from others? Blame them or project our own worst flaws onto them.

Feeling disconnected from nature? Buy a pot plant or watch David Attenborough.

Feeling insecure about your status? Buy a new car or push for a deployment or promotion.

Feeling a lack of purpose? Play a videogame or gamble.

Feeling your past coming back to haunt you? Ignore it and just call it your personality so that you don't have to confront it.

These are all deeply flawed responses to the problems outlined in the "Seven Haiku". I have engaged in all of them except gambling, so I know from experience they don't work and only further the descent into ego, pain, selfishness and disconnection. Though I haven't tried it as a coping strategy, I haven't met many gamblers who see it as the solution to their problems. Gambling releases dopamine and offers short-term relief, and eventually creates another problem. If we truly want to overcome our mental and emotional struggles, we need real solutions, not more chilli.

So, what are real solutions to these seven causes of depression?

Let's look at the first cause, loneliness, as an example. Loneliness is not being alone. We can be alone and enjoy our solitude. Loneliness is not solved by being around people either. We can be in a busy city and feel lonely, or in the mess surrounded by people and feel isolated.

Loneliness is overcome by connection to others with a shared meaning. If we're in a sports team with a shared identity and meaning, there is true connection. If our section, troop, platoon or team have a shared identity and meaning, there is true connection. If we have a partner or close friend who shares our view of the world and values the same things, there is true connection. To overcome loneliness, we need to share more than time and space together; we need to share meaning.

For each of the causes of depression in the "Seven Haiku", there are solutions such as the one above outlined in *Lost Connections*. I address each of the seven causes indirectly throughout this book, so I have not fully unpacked them here. Of these causes, however, I personally believe that the single most important one is our values.

Our values dictate our actions, who we share meaning with, how we connect to the world and nature, the type of work we do, how we treat ourselves, and how secure we are with our status in life.

If you know what your values are, consider whether they are making you depressed and anxious, or if they are helping you to be confident and connect to others. If you are unsure of what your values are, some of the later poems and reflections may help to uncover them.

Lighthouse

Joy bubbles yet solitude springs
in the echoes of my mind
A misty shore as sun passes cliffs
stern to the waters
A shadow outcasts the boy
left behind his sight of a world
endless to a newcomer
Sadness sears in the past of a place not so different
Where the great divide clear cut blue on blue
was the only true certainty
And divinity was attainable in oneself
Where the stone so strong was ever changing,
flawed by the cracks in its facade
And its character ever polished
by the relentless and heartless sea
In the chilling breeze
the harsh vulnerability is inevitable
And the glare stopping you from looking out
forces you to look in
To see the emptiness reflected back
and the insignificance of your presence

Lighthouse – Reflection

"Lighthouse" is a reflection on the idea that nature makes our ego shrink and puts our life into perspective. The infinite expanse of nature forces us to reflect upon the insignificance of our presence.

I wrote this poem about eight years ago while on a training exercise in Jervis Bay, well before I understood what was happening to me. I knew that nature had a way of shrinking my problems, but I had never deliberately approached it for this reason.

Now, nature is one of my most powerful tools that enables me to overcome anxiety and depression. A few hours alone in nature dissolves my worries. I allow myself to be vulnerable to feeling how insignificant my ego really is. This act can be threatening if the identity of our ego is all we have ever known, but it's also liberating if we let go and fully connect with nature.

In the Army, I often found that after a few weeks out field, life became simpler. I was more present and content, and less anxious or depressed. Sure, it was shit at times—the lack of sleep, constant pack marching, and eating nothing but rats get tiring, but just being in nature does incredible things for our mental health.

We evolved to be in nature, not in these concrete jungles we have built. We evolved to be with our tribe, working together to survive in the wild. When we maintain an active connection to both—to nature and to our tribe—we are more whole.

Tribe

I long for some disaster to bring us all together
I long for some new struggle that makes us all unite
It could be a common enemy, or some uncommon threat
It could be our own survival that makes us join the fight

It's not that I want suffering, or don't appreciate this peace
But if safety keeps us separate, then a war would make it right
From the Blitz to Kosovo, the survivors say the same
They long for some old struggle where they held each other tight

Yet war is not the answer, nor pain the only way
We evolved to need this feeling to be part of our tribe
When we feel that we are separate and chase our lonely goals
We bear our struggles heavily, when sharing makes them light

We stepped out from the jungle and survived on the savannah
We spread our clans across the lands and conquered all in sight
Now in this brave new world, with the wilderness at bay
We've lost our tribal nature, which held us through the night

Tribe – Reflection

"Tribe" is a short reflection on the book of the same title by Sebastian Junger. Our experience of leaving the military is not a new or isolated struggle. Junger highlights how issues such as PTSD and suicide are more prevalent in affluent societies lacking in strong communities, traditions and tribal or family units. After service, military members feel this loss of tribe strongly, as we've had the chance to experience what it feels like.

What resonated the most with me from Junger's book is the yearning for some disaster to shake up my reality. Under extreme duress, we can show our true strength and contribute meaningfully to our community. Even in a world where we seldom need to sacrifice ourselves or risk our lives for those we care about, there is still a deep desire to show we are worthy to be here.

Military service, and more specifically, war, provide this opportunity for sacrifice to support the tribe but when we step out into the civilian world, the loss of connection is palpable. When we see people show blatant disregard for the tribe, by littering, stealing or hurting vulnerable people, we feel further isolated. Tribes prevented inequality, yet now we live in societies where millionaires live around the corner from homeless people and may feel no obligation to help. In a platoon setting, we share almost everything. We share food, water, shelter, stories, struggles and meaning. Any act of selfishness in such a group is quickly shunned as being "Jack".

Outside of the military, however, that millionaire may be a veteran, and so too may the homeless person: they just don't know it.

Our connection to our tribe doesn't have to end when we depart the military. On the contrary, I believe we have an added responsibility to instil this sense of tribe into our wider community. We have experienced what it feels like, and we know it makes us more resilient. We each have the chance to create this in our families, our sporting teams, our workplaces, our communities and in our veteran organisations.

Clay

Born as just a ball of clay
Bestowed with all potential
Parents form us in their way
What they believe is essential

School then takes this feeble form
And moulds it to their teaching
Which they themselves were taught "the norm"
The clay will go on preaching

Who decides what's in their minds?
The shape their clay should take
The puppet masters are behind
The "play" that they all fake

Soon it's off to high school where
The moulding charges on
Adolescents playing "truth or dare"
For soon both will be gone

As the clay begins to set
And take its final shape
A life of work they are beset
To navigate red tape

Those that are still malleable
Can dream of "bigger" things
Minds still so impressionable
For university's strings

With so much time to mould the ball
It ends up quite complex
Although it might seem free, in all
It's just a conditioned reflex

The greatest fear of the ruling class
Is that the clay might finally understand
That all its moulding is a farce
And shape itself, by its own hand

Clay – Reflection

"Clay" is a metaphor for how society shapes us, and few are shaped and moulded so thoroughly as those who complete military service. It takes great patience to remould ourselves into who we want to be, and it can be a painful process where we seemingly resist ourselves through our conditioning. We resist change, and just as a smoker trying to quit has to fight inculcated urges, we have to reprogram ourselves not to get angry or talk in acronyms.

Our values are also engrained by our parents, schools, societies and by our service. If these are the values we want to live by, it's acceptable. But if not, what then?

Whist the military provides us with a great sense of tribal belonging, it also changes us in ways that we may need to release. It redefines our values.

It has been over a year since I left the Army, and I still feel unbelievably furious every time my partner makes us late for something. Even though I value her more than I value being on time, my actions say there are still some competing ingrained values. What if the values we have lived by up until now have only made us valuable within the military? What if our values are making us angry, stressed, depressed and anxious?

Take status, for example. If we value admiration or validation from others to prop us up, it is a sure-fire way to become insecure, as status is dependent on extrinsic factors beyond our control. The military is built upon a sense of status, rank, and hierarchy. Yet outside, there is no rank. An overinflated sense of ego quickly bursts once we are no longer in that military context. If we continue to value status, we may become workaholics, or seek another position to satisfy our need for status.

I tried to find every angle to maintain my status after leaving the Army. I was going to travel the world, start a company, become a professor, an inventor, a project manager, or senior design engineer—you name it. If it meant I could hold onto my status, I wanted to do it.

Instead, I spent an entire year unemployed, losing any sense of status. I had to learn to overcome my conditioning, so that I could be myself, and not the clay figure the Army had created out of me. I failed time and again to overcome myself and was humbled by the challenges of being vulnerable. I discovered that what matters most is our values and those we care about, not a false image of ourselves we've created.

There are many other poor values that may be common in veterans and even good military values can cause problems when taken out of context. If we value resilience, for example, we may never allow ourselves to be vulnerable enough to heal old wounds. If we value the actions required for combat, excluding defending our home from a break-in or stopping a fight in the street, this value is not relevant in the outside world.

We are like a pistol, which has been cocked and loaded by our military training and placed in the street. We have been trained to go off when "triggered". We are trained to kill, and value the actions involved in killing. We value the skills of orchestrated death. We value how to maximise our combat power, to plan and synchronise effects to kill the enemy. So how do we transfer these values to the world outside our military experience?

You were taught the brutal truth at the coalface. How to kill as many people as possible in an ambush. How to fire your weapon to greatest effect against the enemy. How to use a bayonet or how to plant claymores. You were trained to value obedience, loyalty, sacrifice, service, honour, courage, and to be an expert in close combat. These values are less likely to help you succeed in the outside world, where self-sacrifice often just leads to being used by an employer, and where being an expert in close combat is either irrelevant or going to get you into trouble.

The military gives us countless invaluable skills, and many of us have specialisations we can take into the future but the underlying skillsets of the soldier are not relevant in civilian society. The values we learned through our service can have a positive impact on our lives and the lives of others, but we need to reframe them for life outside the military.

Take courage, for example. If you value courage, that may mean wanting to be the person who charges the enemy gun pit to save your mates. But seeing courage only from a physical risk standpoint limits the impact this value can have on your life and how you see it expressed in others. This type of courage is rarely needed in modern society outside of disasters, accidents, or violence. By reframing courage as engaging in anything that makes us feel vulnerable, we can expand how much this value can positively impact the world.

People often talk of moral courage—the courage to speak up when you see something that's not right, this is an example of vulnerability. Having the courage to speak up for your values, to do the right thing, to admit mistakes, to share new ideas, or to be your authentic self—all take the courage to be vulnerable.

Our values motivate our actions. We must reframe our values or find values that we want to live by, that we choose for ourselves. Beyond values inculcated by the military, there are many societal values that aren't serving us well. If we value money, for example, there will never be enough. If we value material things, they will fail to satisfy anything deeper in us. If we value independence, we will refuse help and potentially disconnect from others.

If we want to know what we value, we must look at our actions. If we say we value our families, but work late every day, we may actually value our jobs more. If we say we value our health, but eat fast food, drink and binge watch TV, we may actually value pleasure more. If we say we value giving, but delight most when people thank or praise us, we may actually value recognition more. When we observe our actions, we can truly see our values.

Twinkle

A twinkle in an eternal eye
That watches all with nothing judged
Ignored until the end is nigh
Now lost along the path we trudged

We all wander, wither and whine
What should be and what's divine
Too little time for us to season
A lamb in fear without a reason

A tavern calls to quench your thirst
To calm you on your endless search
A life of pleasure is not the worst
But guilt you feel for leaving church

Here in the dim-lit pub, you see
A bearded man with eyes of youth
A twinkle fills your heart with glee
A chance to finally find the truth

What knowledge has the man so wise
That drew you from an endless sleep
Was this the God in plain disguise
That desperate was your heart to keep

"I tell you friend that you are lost
No church or bar or temple needed
You ventured little at such a cost
And never was my warning heeded"

"I am not the God you're seeking
Look at how my skin does wrinkle
I am time, a glimpse you're peeking
Only now and just a twinkle."

Twinkle – Reflection

"Twinkle" is a story of my search for meaning both in and out of the military. Whether we realise it or not, we are all searching for meaning and a purpose throughout our lives. Inside the military, we are told what our values are, how to conduct ourselves, what tasks to do, how to dress, how to look, how to talk, how to think, and what our mission is. There is incredible power in purpose, especially when shared by a team; but when we leave the team, we must face the journey of finding meaning on our own.

If you are aligned with military values and your purpose as part of it, then you can do incredible things as part of the organisation and reap great inner rewards for your efforts. These values and this purpose dictate how we live and who we are, but there are plenty of people and organisations who will happily tell us our purpose so they can get the most out of us.

Marketing tells me that my purpose is to be happy, and that happiness comes from new gadgets, clothes, holidays, experiences or something else external so that I consume more.

Religion tells me that my purpose is to serve a God, to donate to the church and surrender my will to a higher power, which is whatever they interpret it to be.

Bars make me think happiness is in the drink, that I don't need to find meaning in life if I am always numb from alcohol or drugs.

The truth, as far as I can guess, is that no one else can definitively say what our right purpose is. It is something we must come to ourselves, from our own experience. The idea of purpose being found outside of ourselves, or of someone else prescribing it to us is a trap. Our purpose may align with others, and we may be inspired to join other people's missions that we believe in, but no one else can tell us what our purpose should be, true purpose comes from within.

The old man in the poem plays on the idea that there is a wise being out there or within us, whether our superior, role model, god, idol or other person of authority or divinity that can tell us what the meaning of life is. The old man was me finding myself and realising that no bar or temple is needed: I must find my own answer. I am simply a twinkle in an eternal eye, a passing conscious experience of this moment in time, and only wise in the sense that I have accepted the nature of life as ultimately unknowable.

This theme is continued in the next poem, "Galaxies", a further invitation to look within for our own purpose in our lives, based on our own values.

Galaxies

Like galaxies, we swirl around a void
All circling an unknowable emptiness
Not content with this arrangement we avoid
Ever admitting to the depth of our ignorance

False idols make a framework
A way to make sense of reality
For when there is no objective centre
We are compelled to lie for clarity

Faith is the flavour of humanity
For the fervour of the followers
Is founded on their sanity
And the belief that belief holds the key

How do you spin a wheel if you can't agree
On what axis it should revolve?
How do you create progress
Without collective and blind resolve?

It is the burden of Being itself
To look into this void and ask
What am I? What is my purpose?
And never to settle on another's task

Galaxies – Reflection

"Galaxies" is another attempt to highlight the unknowable nature of life, and that we simplify this complexity by making belief structures. By accepting that I don't have the answers to everything, that some aspects of life can never be understood, I am humbled. By understanding too that no one else can know all there is, I am able to trust more my own intuition and my own direction.

Instead of living a life based on existing beliefs, it is far more rewarding to live a life based on values. Beliefs give us a false certainty about what is in the black hole, beyond the knowable universe, when our values are more like the gravity, that keeps us in motion, and aligned with our purpose. True progress is only made when we have a common set of values. This is the axis of the wheel. Our beliefs may be the way we choose to see the world, but our values give a central point to revolve around and in the last stanza, it is the individual's responsibility to find their own centre.

Values

It can be a daunting task to find your own values, and it's very easy to revert to conditioning and what is expected of us to value. Although no one can truly tell us what to value, there are useful frameworks to help us find our own.

In *The Reality Slap,* Dr Harris provides an excellent framework to find our values, proposing three core categories that are essential to any value. He explains how if you boil it down, caring, connection and contribution are at the centre of any value to live a good life. By connecting with others, we feel we belong. By caring for ourselves, others, and the world around us, we can have a positive impact. Through this contribution, our lives gain meaning.

As caring and connection are quite self-explanatory, I will go more in depth into contribution and why it is an important thing to consider when determining your values. In the book, *The Courage to Be Disliked*, it is through contribution that we can derive intrinsic self-worth, otherwise our self-worth is only derived through recognition from others.

We all need a sense of self-worth, but there are two ways to get it. Do we pick up rubbish even if no one is looking, or to be seen as the person who picks up rubbish? Do we act out of values or for validation? For contribution or recognition?

Recognition only compels us to act out of the need for validation, rather than to act out of true values, and this just produces "brown nosers", sycophants and "thrusters". These are very different people to those that excel through passion, dedication, and a sense of purpose, centred on a desire to contribute out of values.

The tall poppy syndrome of the Army is a self-defeating system that stifles passion yet allows for these types of people to thrive as they only pander to the desire for their superiors to be validated. Those who do strive out of a sense of their own values, can end up on the receiving end of "performance punishment" and find themselves overloaded by lazy leadership. Some leaders heap more work on those who consistently perform, rather than investing time in those who need support to improve the collective capability of the team.

It is just like a sand dune: the steepness of the dune is at the exact point that even another grain would cause it to collapse. We run the Army like this, loading people to their breaking points. Some can take a steeper gradient and bear a greater load.

Consider this: if you are one of those overloaded members suffering from performance punishment, are you bearing the load because you value contribution or because you are seeking recognition? If it is the former, and you just care about contributing, then try contributing by helping someone else improve so they can help take the load. If you want the recognition, you will just keep taking the load all to yourself.

If the need to take on more work comes from the sense of being "not good enough", remember that these NGE stories are just that, stories. No amount of work will ever be "good enough". Just do your best. Your best isn't breaking yourself every day, your best is what you can sustain.

If you don't want recognition but fear the reprisal for speaking out about how you are being overloaded, there are people you can talk to. Talk to your peers; talk to your chain of command. If they are unreasonable, talk to your chaplain. If you genuinely express that the workload is unmanageable, it is in their best interest to address it before it reaches a breaking point.

Many of us worry about our Performance Appraisal Report (PAR) coming back negative if we don't cooperate with the expectations placed upon us, but consider what looks better: approaching our superior and asking for mentoring and support so that the job gets done properly, or saying nothing to look infallible until there is a failure point when we cannot handle the work?

We are a team. We are one team. When we put values ahead of recognition and have a true desire to contribute to the team, not a desire for a promotion or deployment, only a fool would punish us for asking for help.

Consider how we could do our job from a place of values, and how those values come back to caring, connection and contribution. If we work from a centre of values, we can start to address the issues of tall poppy syndrome, performance punishment and thrusting, and create a more inclusive culture that aspires to a collective excellence, not individual success.

Tall Poppy

We often joke "Never be first
Never be last, and never volunteer"
Well, if you served, you volunteered
You offered yourself to endure the worst

Some naive Lewy, crusty WO
Dargin or even digger may say
"Thank you for your service", though
They're not the words they mean to convey

Tall Poppies cut, row on row
Till all the soldiers stunted grow
For such a symbolic flower we mock
Anyone who shows pride in the flock

In however long your service was
And no matter the situations you faced
You chose to work for a higher cause
For that your pride should be embraced

Tall Poppy – Reflection

"Tall Poppy" calls us to stop the culture of undermining the value of our service, stop undermining those with skill and passion, those with pride and a desire to serve. The phrase, "Thank you for your service", is practically an insult among military members, almost akin to being "Champed". Why?

A colleague once said, "We are all happy to slag on the military with each other, to complain and be jaded, but the moment we go home for a Christmas BBQ and someone asks what it's like, we all swell up with pride."

It's fine to carry on and be jaded, but it's an enormous challenge when we leave and are no longer able to draw a sense of pride from belonging to the military. Without that identity, we are reliant on the memory of our service to feel a sense of pride.

After my departure from the military, I struggled to feel I had rendered effective service. Since then, however, I have had contact with soldiers who have thanked me genuinely for supporting them. This knowledge made the time worth it for me. Even if I did not deploy, I know my service mattered.

If you can support a mate, or someone struggling through the hardship of service, then you have served well. If you serve with passion and do not let the tall poppy syndrome cut you down, you have served well. If you served until you were broken by the military—physically or mentally—you gave more than most people ever do in their lifetime to a cause, whether or not it was warlike service.

Heroes

For a thousand eyes a blinded crowd
Deceived will drown in lies and doubt
A shroud of fear is ever clear
The noise that masks the master's spout

Pouring in the roaring sin
The general din, delight, and grin
Severing the final skin
Uncovering disguise and spin

Please ignore the truth once more
It's better for your health to store
Your wealth for war, than test the law
Lest you pick the shortest straw

You rooted for the underdog
A paradox, for such a cog
In the machine that you believe
Double think what hero means

Who goes against the social norm
Is vilified for breaking form
Yet through the storm, the martyr's born
Hindsight's heroes that we mourn

Heroes – Reflection

"Heroes" reflects on the idea that the people we worship from the past were often the ones most persecuted in their time for going against common beliefs. It's ironic how we always root for the underdog in movies, yet in reality, we punish them for speaking out or being different. It is only in hindsight that we can see their virtues.

The "thousand eyes" that are "blinded" is the group think that stops people from seeing the truth. "Double think" refers to the concept from George Orwell's *1984*, in which it was normal to hold two conflicting beliefs in one's mind simultaneously. Fear keeps people silent and obedient, allowing them to hold conflicting beliefs.

Like the phrase "thank you for your service" or "champ", "hero" is another term that gets used to insult people for doing the right thing. There are many heroes amongst our veterans, many who have suffered greatly to help out their mates, though they would never call themselves a hero. I believe there are many more doing the work to change the culture and make the Army a better place. They too may never be recognised.

The culture of using fear to control people is outdated and it is time we move to an organisation that truly encourages initiative. As mentioned in "Throwing Stones", marksmanship coaches would often just yell at the firers, whereas now with the new culture around marksmanship training, soldiers are taught to be comfortable and confident around their weapon. This initiative will not only improve the discriminate use of force within our military but will also reduce training incidents where soldiers are unnecessarily losing their lives.

Our Anzacs came from the country. They were farmers and they knew their way around a firearm, harsh bushland, and extreme weather. They were also known for their cunning, innovation, and initiative. It is this confidence in hardship that we should be building, this adaptability that we should encourage, incorporating strength together, rather than fear or competition.

Not everyone can be pinned with a Victoria Cross, nor may we ever live up to the Anzac legend, but we can stand up for what we believe in and try our best to make the Army a better organisation. Everyone has a chance to overcome their own vulnerability, to show their initiative, and to offer their own unique strength.

Often, we consider our heroes to be those who show great courage, yet we see vulnerability as weakness. One of my favourite lines on courage is by Brené Brown from her book *The Power of Vulnerability*, and it is used to reach military members who believe vulnerability is weakness. She simply asks them to "Think of one example of courage without vulnerability".

Trauma

I wish I knew how to help you
I wish I had the answers then
But I was naive, young and new
If only I had that time again

What do you say to someone who
Has trauma beyond your comprehension?
How do you help them make it through
To escape their pain and apprehension?

I'd heard about this many times
But our training doesn't really teach
Of ways to heal things of the mind
Or how to help those you can't reach

What is PTSD to me?
When I have no idea of war
How could I help him to be free
From the horrors that he saw

Although I know I can't relate
There are still ways I could have helped
And if you read this, it's not too late
To offer help to someone else

What saved me from my own mind
Was not the psych or medication
It was the books she helped me find
That freed me from my isolation

If you know someone in pain
Or if that someone you know is you
Never underestimate the gain
From reading books to help you through

Trauma – Reflection

I wrote "Trauma" to highlight the feeling of helplessness when we do not know how to support someone with trauma or PTSD, and the immense benefits of reading books to better understand it, for ourselves and others. Beyond the techniques outlined in "Soliloquy" to release stored emotions and trauma, there are many more techniques available in an extremely powerful book that has changed my life and the lives of others around me.

The Body Keeps the Score by Bessel van der Kolk is a psychology book that explains the many ways in which our body stores memory, emotions, and trauma, often without our conscious awareness of it. The book covers in detail many different treatment methods for PTSD that do not rely on prescription drugs.

Although I never suffered PTSD, I had soldiers under my command who did. Trying to help them as their troop commander, I felt useless. Even with the support of psychologists, psychiatrists, medical specialists, and rehabilitation managers, some of the cases were near impossible to help. All I could do was give the person space.

I read this book to help me understand ways to deal with my own issues, and in the process, I found many tools and techniques that would have been useful if I had read them as a troop commander.

As this book covers so many techniques, it is something you must read yourself if you want to get the full benefits to take back control of your life, or if you want to understand better how to help others.

Consider the story of the storeroom in the mansion. This book has many keys, but we each have different rooms to unlock, and the keys to freedom may be in another book. If you're struggling with trauma, maybe the next key is in *The Body Keeps the Score*. Trauma can be covert and may be disguised as frustration at work or with a partner, social isolation, anger, guilt, shame, or sadness. It may be disguised as the perpetual sense of not being good enough, those NGEs, or it may just be that we have triggers that are unconsciously avoided.

Not everyone who is reading this will have PTSD, though there are many who do, and may never have acknowledged it. It can be hard to admit we have an issue if we don't know how to resolve it, but we can't begin to heal until we identify our problem. There are solutions out there, and the dive into treatment isn't as daunting when we know there are ways to heal.

Concepts like Post Traumatic Growth (PTG) show that PTSD is not an unsolvable lifelong issue, but rather, can be the source of great strength once understood, managed, and treated. Beyond just the stigma of getting help, I personally had the fear that once I opened the floodgates, my life would fall apart. But as I reached out, the raging torrent of emotions subsided.

If you don't let anything out, even a steady rain will eventually burst the dam and release everything at once. Reaching out is a way to release the pressure and lower the water level, without destroying everything downstream.

After reaching out, the emotions became more like reading the tides for me, than like riding through rapids. Only we know what's being held behind the dam wall. From the outside, it looks like concrete right until the moment it breaks or begins to leak.

If you have mates who have highlighted issues and concerns for you—if they are noticing the leaks—it is worth talking to someone before the wall breaks.

Anxiety

How subtle is anxiety
A thought, a fear, the air
Surrounded by the invisible,
A sort of clear despair

I breathe it in, fills my blood
It flows into my veins
Quickly goes my heart racing
To avoid impending pain

Yet nothing happens, no one's hurt
The fear is just a ruse
Despite the fact it wasn't real
The thoughts did leave a bruise

It sticks like quicksand
And grips me sinking
The more I fight
The more trapped my thinking

And soon I find my mind has gone
In circles spinning far beyond
I've lost control and roll and spin
And spiral down to burn in sin

What was the thought that triggered me
To collapse my whole world inwardly?
Something now so trivial
In hindsight that it's laughable

When you feel anxiety's pull
Create some space to see in full
The situation from afar
And realise just how strong you are

Feel your fears as just a book
In your face there's nowhere to look
But placed upon your lap it's clear
It's just a book, nothing to fear

That's not to say to hold away
The book at arm's length just to stay
At peace with it when all it does
Is tire you and kill your buzz

Neither hide the book behind
Your back or else it will remind
Your mind there's something still repressed
And all we hide must be expressed

It's best to rest the book in view
Relaxed upon your lap review
The words and thoughts as one small part
Of a greater world within your heart

We are not our thoughts and minds
Nor are we our anxious binds
We are the higher consciousness
Aware of this experience

Anxiety – Reflection

"Anxiety" came to me when I was in its grip. I was sitting in a café when all kinds of anxious thoughts came to my mind of the millions of things that could go wrong in my life.

"I still don't have a job."

"I don't have my own home."

"I don't know what I want to do."

"I've lost my sense of purpose."

And there were many more things I worried about all at once.

Until my psychologist identified the anxiety, I just thought it was normal to think the way I did. I've always been told I overthink things, but this overthinking is what propelled me through my education and military training.

I was told I worry too much, but again, I justified this as being prepared. When faced with uncertainty, we all try to prepare by predicting what will happen. It is the same thing when we conduct military planning. Whilst this can be helpful if preparing for a new and difficult task with a lot of uncertainty such as planning military operations, it becomes toxic when applied in excess in every waking moment.

The below section covers useful tools, resources and perspectives to help manage and overcome anxiety.

Worry and Rumination

My psychologist recommended a great resource during our time together, the workbook *What? Me Worry?* Follow the website link in the reference section for help rewiring the brain to engage less in worry and rumination.

The workbooks on this website are simple, but effective and I recommend them to anyone with a stressful job, even if anxiety isn't an issue. For those who have a partner or friend who may be struggling with anxiety, the workbooks can be helpful as well. My partner and I each did the workbook and it helped her understand what I was making an effort to address.

Another exercise outlined in this poem is taken from Dr Harris' book as a way to put NGEs, worries or other negative thought patterns into perspective. If we hold our negative thoughts before us like a book, they are everywhere we look. We can't see anything else, and we can't put them into perspective. When we put our thoughts behind us to try and ignore them, they manifest in more insidious, unconscious ways and eventually slip into our minds. When we try resist them, they drain us. But the fourth way is simply allowing the thoughts to be, like a book in our lap—a small part of our present experience.

If you're worrying about something, try to imagine the worries as just a small book on your lap, as only one aspect of this present moment. Then ask these questions:

Is this worrying helping me?

What beliefs do I have that make me think worrying is good?

What is the worst consequence of my worries and what would I do to deal with that event?

What do I value that makes me worry about this situation?

What action can I take now, that is in line with my values?

For another angle, return to the story of the storeroom and imagine anxiety as being glued to the TV. Even with the keys to leave that tiny room, we can still get lured back in by the stories on our TV: our repetitive thoughts.

Creating space, or expanding our awareness is the process of letting go of what is on TV and once again walking out of the storeroom, the mansion and into the gardens, where we can again see the TV, the anxiety, as one small part of our whole conscious experience.

Another perspective that helped me appeared while I was looking for work after the Army. I had been offered a paid Ph.D. scholarship at a neuroscience institute at the University of Queensland and one of the topics deeply resonated with me. There is a growing theory in neuroscience that our brains are just a predictive coding machine that seeks to minimise prediction errors. In this model, emotions are simply there to highlight a prediction error so that we don't forget them.

When we think about it, we feel surprised by unexpected events, sadness from sudden losses, and anger toward unwanted surprises. When our mind does not correctly predict certain events, specific emotions are elicited.

Even laughter can occur with the unexpected. If someone's hat blows off on parade, the prediction error is funny for you and embarrassing for them. In both cases, the emotional response highlights the prediction error so that next time you are on parade and it's windy, your updated prediction model has you pushing your chin into the strap.

But anxiety is when we think we're on parade 24/7. The wind feels like it could come out of nowhere and no matter how much we try to anticipate what might happen, something will still catch us by surprise. We constantly tense our jaws and check our straps, listen for the wind, and look around cautiously.

If this model is right, then the way we predict what will happen each moment is entirely shaped by our past experiences. In many ways then, our lives before we joined the military have shaped how we respond to our service. Our upbringing shapes our attachment style and how we engage in intimate relationships, as well as how we define ourselves, set boundaries and what we think we deserve in life. Our anxiety may appear to be in response to the high stress nature of our jobs, but the roots may go deeper.

It's important to explore not just what issues we have during and after service, but also those buried so deep we may have forgotten about them. This is covered in the poem "Meditation", as caring for the inner child. Even these deep seated and seemingly immovable issues can be resolved.

With the tools outlined in this section, I can put my

issues into perspective and realise what's shaped me in the past. Our hats blowing off is not the end of the world. Once we have healed our past, we can look to the present. We can see that we are safe. We are loved. We can accept ourselves as we are. We are able see the world as it is, as opposed to how we expect it to be.

When we stop seeing the world as a prediction based on experience, we allow new possibilities into our lives. If our lives are playing on the TV in the storeroom, all we will ever see is based on past experiences. Becoming truly present allows us to see the world as it is, not just how we think it is.

If you're still struggling with worries or anxiety, the poem "Meditation" may offer clarity. "Meditation" allows us to move freely around the mansion and the gardens, to walk back outside for fresh air and a fresh perspective.

Coffee Snobs

It started with a sachet of the old Blend 43
And evolved beyond Nescafe to make better bush coffee
I trialled Moccona Classic, then the famous Robert Timms
And even hand ground coffee in an AeroPress with skim

But none of these would satisfy the thirst or growing need
So I smuggled in my trusty old Nespresso pod machine
We ran it from the genny with a second-hand bar fridge
Yet soon we had been beaten by some civvies on the ridge

On the hills above Shoalwater, with TS raging on
Sat an AAFCANS truck surrounded by the addicts gazing on
It hit me in that moment, that I was not alone
We've become a bunch of coffee snobs, a title that we own

Coffee Snobs – Reflection

As much as I love coffee, I put this poem after the section on anxiety, as it is a dangerous combination when we are stressed or anxious. We all love a good brew, but we've become a coffee obsessed culture. It's a social addiction that mediates a break or an excuse to leave the office.

I've always been prone to stress, and my coffee obsession hasn't helped. If you are finding yourself more susceptible to stress or anxiety, consider cutting back on the caffeine. Whilst our anxiety may be caused by our circumstances as outlined in the "Seven Haiku", implementing the techniques to overcome it can be harder when we are over-caffeinated.

Bad Investment

Our most precious resource is our time
So where do we invest it?
Attention is the only sign
Of where it is directed

For we could sit for hours
In the sun out on the sand
Oblivious to the ocean
While we try to understand

Some wildly insignificant
Or meaningless detail
Of an argument we had one day
Or a moment where we failed

It's just like compound interest
Where these thoughts do multiply
By the time that we've invested
Till our debts have grown sky high

But like a sunken cost
We continue adding time
In a desperate attempt to save
The losses in our mind

So sell it at a loss
In a chance to save your soul
And begin to reinvest
In the things that make you whole

I've heard that gratitude
Yields incredible results
And just like contribution
There's a growth you cannot fault

In the words of Warren Buffett
"When they're greedy we'll be fearful"
And "when they're fearful we'll be greedy"
Though their money we're not here for

For it's time that people take
And try to make their own
Even though it's ours at stake
They will make us get a loan

But don't believe the hype
For it's one thing we cannot borrow
So don't try to sell today
For some illusion of tomorrow

Spend it in the present
In each moment passing by
With attention our investment
For a better yield in life

Bad Investment – Reflection

"Bad Investment" is a metaphor for where we place our attention in life. We can be at the beach, yet in our minds we are at work, in the past, in the future or focused on some other distraction from the present. It's like an investment with interest, as it seems the longer that we focus on bad things from our past, the bigger they become, and the harder they are to stop thinking about.

The same goes for positive thoughts or attention invested in the present moment. When we focus on the things that we are grateful for, they not only become more important to us, but they also give us more joy.

Also like an investment, we think we have to sacrifice our time now for some future gain in interest. But time never gets more interesting than it is now. It is only affected by the degree of attention we give it. We make our future better not by sacrificing our time, but by investing it in the "now".

I'm not saying we should suddenly spend all of our money on different pleasures to "live in the moment", but rather, that we should invest our attention now, if we want to have a better present and a better future.

If we are trying to hit a target, it doesn't help to think about all the times that we missed in the past, or how good we will be in the future if we hit it. The only thing that will make us successful in the moment is to focus our attention on hitting it. Then we practice over and over, each time being present as the shot is released.

We can't plan to be good at something in the future, we can only make progress now. Likewise, we can't plan to enjoy ourselves. We are either enjoying ourselves in a moment, or we are not. Happiness is not something we save up for, it is a by-product of being present, of being grateful for what we have and enjoying the moment.

If a moment is terrible, it still doesn't help to escape by thinking about the past or the future. If we are in danger, then that moment demands all of our attention. If we are afraid, then again, we need to practice courage, which requires presence to overcome that fear. If the moment is terrible simply because it is unenjoyable, then it is a chance to observe why we dislike it, so we can work towards removing it from our lives if possible. It may be that we dislike it because the situation exposes our weaknesses.

If we don't enjoy things because we are not good at them, being present in that moment could give us the chance to improve. Visualising the future can be a great tool to help align our practice, but if we are looking to improve in some area, then we still need to do the hard work now.

Eckhart Tolle, in his book titled *The Power of Now,* highlights the nature of psychological time as separate from physical time. Wherever there is psychological time, such as past and future in our minds, we are separate from our reality or physical time, which is always now.

Problems arise when we see our situations solely from our minds, rather than for what they actually are. For example, if I broke my leg, this is not a problem objectively; it is a situation. It is my personal or subjective opinion that labels my situation as a problem. Psychological time creeps in when we think of the past and how we broke our leg, or when we fear for a future where it may not get better.

The following poem "Suffering" talks about this perspective shift and the reflection covers the story of my struggle when I was unable to see my life from a place of presence or gratitude.

Suffering

Is suffering an ordeal or subjective?
Is pain any more real or objective?
It seems fear plays a part, it's selective
And hope frees us a path, gives perspective

From stubbed toes to head blows, they're relative
Without meaning my foot needs a sedative
But a broken nose is a joke if its competitive
It seems purpose plays part in the reflexive

And what of hunger and grief a real experience
You miss lunch and question your own resilience
Then there's people who starve and beg forgiveness
And those who pray to their god with only willingness

What sets them apart from our own suffering?
It's clear their life's worse, there's not enough for them
Yet they are grateful for whatever their life is offering
They give thanks for the plate, now is that suffering?

Now grief, you repeat that it is painful
But one's death is a gate; we make it meaningful
In some cultures, they dance and sing, it's beautiful
It's our choice that we view it as something mournful

If grief, pain, and hunger can inspire
Why is it so many avoid their fire?
It seems we choose to be slaves to our own desires
Despite the fact it's our struggles that growth requires

Take time to abstain from one compulsion
Create space for your mind to find devotion
Allow your body to groan, express emotion
And see your consciousness grow in an explosion

Without the noise of desire as your distraction
Or fear of suffering guiding you to reaction
Escape the limited mind and its contraction
You'll find freedom to choose your every action

Suffering – Reflection

“Suffering” highlights how personal and subjective pain and suffering can be. I’ve kept training with a broken nose and pack marched on a broken foot, we’ve all pushed through such pain when required. Despite the injuries, my sense of purpose and belief kept me focused on something that surpassed pain.

When we complete intense physical training, our back may ache, our heart may pound, and our legs may feel like they’re about to give way, but we can push through this pain with a strong sense of purpose and firm belief. A purpose makes the pain worth it, and we can believe that through the pain, we become stronger.

The following section is an extension of this poem’s reflection, and a deep dive into pain, a central theme of this book and my experience.

In Plain Sight – Pain and Insight

As mentioned under the poem "Suffering", addressing pain is central to this book. The play on words with the cover to also read as "Pain and Insight" illustrates the deep link between the two.

This is a longer, somewhat intense section of the book, but something I consider essential. We all go through pain and injury at various points in our lives, and for some medically discharged members, it's quite an ordeal. Any knowledge to make it easier is worth our time.

The below story does not serve as medical advice but is a personal account of my struggle with pain and injury along with the knowledge that helped me through it. I do not intend to undermine the medical system here in any way, only to say that it is always worth conducting our own research when it comes to our treatment.

When I was suffering the worst of the pain from my back injury, some days I collapsed in tears when I got home. I would lie on the floor in pain, unable to move without sharp pains stabbing through my lower back. I had pulses of tingling, itchiness, numbness then pain running down my leg from the sciatica, followed by locking of the muscles in my calf, hamstring and lower back. Sometimes the tension was too much to stand or sit.

What helped me was not treatment, but knowledge from books. Understanding that discs can regenerate, the body can heal itself, that medications didn't help my body repair itself, and that pain is a neurological phenomenon which can be managed, all helped me to overcome this condition to a stage where I can self-manage.

There is a growing body of research that shows anti-inflammatories slow down the healing of injuries. When you take anti-inflammatories, they mask the pain and reduce swelling, removing the very liquid required to heal the injury. When we take other painkillers, we might continue doing the wrong movements that add to the damage. Rest can also limit repair, as with some back injuries the vertebrae must move to allow for the fluid to flow.

My greatest healing and overcoming of the pain didn't come from a physio program, but rather, from the psychologist. She recommended *Explain Pain* by David Butler and Lorimer Moseley, two Australian researchers: a physiotherapist and a neuroscientist. This book taught me to understand how pain is a warning signal and not necessarily indicative of damage. It is something that grows when we fear it. When we focus on it, we intensify its importance and our sensitivity to it, and when we try to suppress it, it grows louder. When we accept pain as another sensation in our body, it can be understood and managed in a similar way to anxiety. Though I've had pain which makes anxiety seem trivial, the two are connected and can be addressed through common techniques. With the right pain management, it can be a book on your lap, only one part of your whole experience.

Explain Pain is a life changing book. If you're suffering from pain, please get this book. Every RAP waiting room, every physio's office and every on base gym should get a copy of *Explain Pain*, it is a life saver.

Once I understood the nature of pain and that the body could heal, I strived to learn how to heal it faster. Another critical book which helped me to heal was *The Biology of Belief* by Dr Bruce Lipton, a researcher in epigenetics, who highlights that our DNA structure changes in response to our perceptions of our environment. Our perceptions are shaped by our beliefs, so our beliefs affect how we heal.

One example he uses is how we would respond to seeing a snake. If as a kid you were taught to fear snakes, they evoke a fight or flight response when encountered. If as a kid your parents taught you to understand and respect snakes, even how to hold them, when you encounter one, you might not fear the snake, but instead only look at it with curiosity and respect. Our beliefs shape our perceptions; our perceptions shape our DNA; and our DNA shapes every process in our bodies.

Our belief shapes whether our body is in a state of stress or in a state or recovery, in a state of restlessness or restfulness. Our belief about pain makes us suffer and avoid it or persevere and grow through it.

Consider the placebo effect. Our belief that something will heal us alters how well we heal. The placebo effect is so powerful that placebos must be used in controlled trials of new treatment methods and substances to ensure the new method is healing the patient, not just their belief in its healing effects. In other words, we can create the placebo effect, and we can heal ourselves when we believe we are being healed.

Once I left the Army, I approached a new physio outside

of Defence. He taught me new strategies that tied in perfectly with both *Explain Pain* and *The Biology of Belief*. In fact, he had a copy of *Explain Pain* on his shelf. The two main concepts he showed me were "The Rattlesnake" and "Load vs Capacity".

In the first concept, our belief about pain is just like the belief about snakes. Imagine pain is the sound of a rattlesnake's tail. To grow stronger, we must push through some amount of pain: the "rattle zone", where we can hear the snake's rattle, but there's no real danger yet.

If we are exercising and there is no pain at all, no rattle, it's not doing us any good. If we're in a small amount of pain while lifting heavy weights at the gym, aching from a long run, or the heart is pounding from high cardio load, then we are in the rattle zone. There is a small amount of pain, but no danger. The closer to the snake you get, the louder the rattle, and greater the pain and training value.

What we need to respect is the strike zone, the point where the snake can strike and put us out of action. If we surpass the strike zone and get bitten, i.e., do not respect our own limits and get injured, we must recover from the injury before returning to the rattle zone to continue training. Eventually rehabilitation requires us to go back to the rattle zone to rebuild strength.

If we fear snakes, however, we will avoid the rattle zone and won't recover or regain strength after an injury. When we know the rattle is just a sound, and respect the limit of our capacity, we can rehabilitate ourselves. The old expression "once bitten twice shy" applies here. If we hurt our back doing deadlifts, we're more likely to avoid them or tense up when trying them again, even before reaching our actual limit.

This pattern prevents effective rehab and we become more susceptible to injury from both the tension and avoidance. If we have been bitten by the rattlesnake—be it an ACL, labral tear, bulged disc, or sprained ankle—eventually, we must confront the injury once it has recovered enough and go back to the rattle zone and experience some pain in our rehab.

A lot of what prevents effective recovery is the mind's limits. I know for myself after having so many recurring back injuries, I didn't want to touch deadlifting or any strenuous back exercise. I would get pain with the slightest weight, as my whole body would tense in anticipation and I would stress having the "perfect form", so I didn't risk reinjury. But surely enough, I still injured myself.

The second concept shows that injury is less about form, and more a matter of load vs capacity. Here load is the training intensity, weight or distance, and capacity is our current level of capability. If you have recently injured your knee, and return to weighted squats, it doesn't matter if you have the perfect form, if your capacity is not yet able to bear the load, you risk reinjury. Even the idea of a straight back for a deadlift is just a matter of load vs capacity. For a large load, a straight back will manage better but the body can be trained to take load even with a curved spine.

Take one look at weightlifters doing 60kg Jefferson curls (a completely curved back deadlift) from a deficit and you will see that the back can be under load while bent. It is all just about load vs capacity. Capacity can be increased by form, but it can also be decreased by unnecessary tension. Capacity can also be decreased by lack of sleep, dehydration, hangover, stress, injury, illness, or other health factors. The fear of using our back and the need to use it "perfectly" create the tension that leads to reinjury, as we do not train the muscles.

If the load is too far below capacity, there is atrophy. If the load is at capacity, there is maintenance. If the load just exceeds the capacity, in the rattle zone, there is growth. If the load is far in excess of the capacity—the strike zone—there is injury. If we believe an exercise will hurt us, we're more likely to tense up, strain and resist the activity and hurt ourselves by trying to perfect the movement.

Whilst I still occasionally suffer bouts of pain, limited range of motion, stiffness, weakness or back spasms, I can still engage in activities I couldn't imagine before leaving the Army. Since transitioning, I have returned to running, hiking with a pack, and even rock climbing. I know that much like anxiety and depression, the pain will rear its ugly head from time to time, but I know how to manage it now, and I know it will recover.

Applying these techniques, I completed the Kokoda Challenge again in 2021, beating my previous time by over an hour and forty minutes, and finishing without any injuries. There was still pain for almost the entire 96km, but I knew what was within my limits and that the pain didn't mean danger.

The first time I tried this challenge in 2018 with a team from my troop, we ran about 5km at the start, and three of our four teammates finished with injuries, one of them being me. We didn't respect our limits, and though we were faster at the start, early fatigue led to injury which slowed us down for the rest of the course. This is another reason to see injury as a function of load vs capacity.

Some injuries will never heal, and we must be accepting of ourselves if we are no longer capable of working or doing activities that we used to. But injury does not exempt us from having to try where we can, to grow through pain, and do whatever is in our power to manage it. We must learn to face and overcome our pain, not for the sake of serving the ego or meeting other people's expectations, but for our own self-worth, health and quality of life.

Just as pain becomes active well before our physical limit and risk of injury so too does our sense of suffering. We can suffer before something has happened, or in anticipation of something happening. Injuries can make us suffer at the thought of being weak or broken in some way. We can fear failure before even engaging in a task and suffer before anything happens.

Suffering, like pain, has a rattle zone—a point where suffering is just a sound in our ear, a fear or anxiety. Suffering becomes real when we actually get hurt or lose something or someone dear to us. But even then, the suffering can be far less intense in reality than what we conjured up in our heads. We can suffer for a sick loved one who we fear may not live much longer, and the fear of losing them is greater and longer than their actual passing. Often too, we suffer when we suppress our emotions to avoid showing vulnerability when we are injured or experience loss.

With our losses, we can always choose how we respond. We can experience the loss of someone dear and we can celebrate the life they lived. We cannot always control our initial response, and if we must mourn, we can mourn fully. Just like taking painkillers, repression never works. Just like tensing before a heavy lift, we are more likely to suffer a mental injury by avoidance, tensing up and holding back our deepest emotions.

When we understand the belief or perspective that underlies our emotion, we can release it. If we are suffering the potential loss of a loved one, for example, the emotion may be wrapped in the urge to express how we feel about them in the time they have left. If our emotions are from fear of reinjury, perhaps we don't want to be vulnerable in other people's eyes, or we're afraid we'll be medically discharged. Our beliefs give rise to the suffering in the rattle zone.

If we believe missing a meal will make us starve, we'll feel anger and will suffer. If we know we can go a full week with almost no food, we won't fret at a day's hunger. If we believe all pain means damage, we will avoid rehab. If we believe that pain is necessary for growth, then we won't fear it during rehabilitation. If we believe that life ends when we leave the military, we will suffer the fear of being discharged. If we believe leaving the military will be the start of a new life however, we'll be grateful for fresh opportunities and find purpose in the pain of transitioning. In short, if we don't believe in ourselves and lose hope for the future, any mistake, loss or change can be shattering. If we do believe in ourselves and that through our struggles we can grow, there is hope in every hardship.

To overcome suffering, we must overcome responding to the world through reaction or repression, attraction or aversion. We need to rise above the impulses of desire and fear.

Consider this: do you act upon the world or react to it? If you feel hunger and you eat, it's a reaction. If you fear something and avoid it, it's a reaction. If you feel pain and abandon a task, it's a reaction. Whether the carrot or the stick, we can determine when we are driven by fear or drawn by desire.

The alternative is to be driven from within—by purpose and values—and to choose the right actions regardless of if they cause suffering in the short term. We can hold the belief that life will get better if we strive through the pain. While life is full of suffering, we can overcome it by acting upon the world through values, rather than just reacting to fears and desires.

Key to managing injury, pain, and emotional struggles is belief. Our beliefs shape how we experience pain, influence how we heal, and shape what we feel.

Our beliefs, values and purpose are inextricably linked. We cannot have one without the others.

How do we know what we value and what our purpose is? We need clarity and gain it by abstaining from desires and overcoming fears. Just as described in the earlier poem "Galaxies", we choose for ourselves what this purpose is and what we value. The later poem "Meditation" gives a method to find this clarity.

It is important to note here that finding your purpose and your values is a continual and lifelong task. Encountering challenges in health or losing a loved one can shift our values. Having children also completely shifts our values. Even realising our greatest success can ring hollow and cause a sudden shift in our values.

It can be a struggle to find a sense of purpose and uncover our values. If we find ourselves adopting the values of a group without question, we can ask if these really are our values, and if not, why? And if we feel a lack of purpose, we can seek ways to improve the world immediately around us.

We are not short of work to be done.

Even a smile has a purpose.

Privilege

There is wisdom in silence
For in it we can hear
The guiding voice of our conscience
And the whisper of the wind in our ear

There is power in stillness
As we all move too fast
To see the hour through busy-ness
It creates space to grow from our past

There is strength in vulnerability
If we have the courage to let go
Of our pride and our dignity
We can let our heart truly show

There is love in sadness
When we look behind the tears
They come from a place of gladness
That we shared so many of the years

There is purpose in pain
For it calls us to arms
To grow through the strain
And find the rainbow when the storm calms

There is privilege in loss
For to lose is to have shared
A connection worth the cost
Where you loved and deeply cared

There is freedom in acceptance
It's through surrender we find atonement
And we allow ourselves forgiveness
To bring us to this present moment

There is presence in absence
If our light we have shone
In that stillness and silence
We are never alone

Privilege – Reflection

I wrote "Privilege" to say goodbye to my Nan when she recently passed away. I also wrote it to help support my family as they struggled with the loss and grief. The theme of "strength in vulnerability" from "Black Cloud" has helped me through. Knowing that it takes greater strength to show our vulnerability than to hide it can give us the courage to grieve.

By refusing to label feelings as good or bad, we can process and let go of them. By processing our pain, we can support our family and mates through theirs.

As I mentioned under "Suffering", if you must mourn, mourn fully. By processing the pain, we can return to a sense of privilege for the chance to share our lives with those we care about, even in their absence.

Dawn

In the cold of morning is our best hour
Reborn, forgiven, renewed, restored
The fog on a lake or the dew on a flower
There's a calm and stillness, the true reward

The burden of life, not yet bestowed
Leaves a space for being, without expectation
The freedom to live, the debt of this ode
When we gather together, each year as a nation

It's not just the chill of the air in our lungs
That sends shivers pouring down through our core
It's the truth of something on the tip of our tongues
That this spirit endures, more than each war

For all of the horrors that man has inflicted
All of the pain and struggles that come
Each war has ended, yet we've always reflected
That their courage and mateship would never succumb

There's something timeless about selfless giving
Something inspiring in each sacrifice
That to gather one morning to pause how we're living
Opens our hearts to heed their advice

Don't take it for granted, it could end tomorrow
It could be the last time you see the sun rise
Don't wait for the moment you lose all you borrow
And return to dust and say your goodbyes

Grab those you love and hold them in tight
Thank them for all they have done from your heart
And in the silence, before the morning light
Honour the spirit our Anzacs impart

Dawn – Reflection

There is something about the Dawn Service that cannot be put into plain words, it can only be felt. "Dawn" is an attempt to express how we can use this feeling to honour those that have gone before, by bringing their mateship, courage, and sacrifice into our lives.

There is no point unpacking this poem further here. I'm sure you know the feeling.

Last year was my first Anzac Day since leaving the military, and it couldn't have been a starker contrast. What was previously a Dawn Service surrounded by fellow soldiers, officers, veterans and family, followed by marching then beers and two-up, was instead a day spent completely alone. I've refrained from mentioning the COVID 19 pandemic in this book as I didn't want to distract from the journey everyone faces when leaving, regardless of the global situation. It was, however, also central to my struggle, like it was for many others on this particular Anzac Day.

I woke up at 5am in the spare room on Mum's property: a small block of land, surrounded by beautiful countryside. As I went to leave the house alone, her dog Bryan, a large, clumsy German Shephard came bounding after me. As we walked through the long grass, the dew from the night soaked my pants and boots, and the chill of the darkness set in.

I reached for my hat, but I wasn't wearing one. I stood there, silent, staring out over the hills, at the fog settled in the gully below. Bryan, noticing the sense of occasion, sat staring straight ahead with me. I imagined the sound of the bugle and the ode. I listened to the silence grow. I reflected on all the Anzac Days passed, and on my service too and just as I began to tear up at the isolation from that once strong identity, the birds began to sing. At first it was the eastern whipbird that cracked out of the silence. Then the carolling of the magpies, and the kookaburras too until the whole valley echoed with their songs.

In that moment, I felt more connected than ever to that identity. To the land. To our nature. I imagined the many Anzacs that lived on farms just like this, who heard the birds sing, and who went off to war to protect this beauty we now share.

Birds

I am in the call of a currawong
The magpie and the crow
The squawking of a cockatoo
And the whipbird's echo

I am in the morning silence
And the moment that it breaks
When the cacophony of kookaburras
Laugh as the day wakes

I am in the vibrant colours
Of a wattle, gold in bloom
In the crimson of the bottlebrush
And their delicate perfume

I am the shadow of the ghost gum
That cools the mob of roos
And the gentle breeze that's blowing
While the koala has a snooze

I am in the raging torrents
From the floods of seasonal rain
And even in red deserts
Where the sun gives no refrain

I have been for generations
In the rock of Uluru
In the shifting sands of coastlines
That eternally renew

And if you stand upon my shores
You are part of this great being
A custodian of harmony
To keep all our birds singing

Birds – Reflection

"Birds" is a poem about responsibility, about our home and what we defend. Australia is many things to many people, but to me, it is a refuge of nature and harmony. It is a way of living and a set of values. It is a place that anyone from any country may call home and be welcomed, but it is also a place that carries with it a responsibility, a custodianship, and one that demands a respect for nature.

There are so many ways the Australian bushland and wildlife can kill you, and yet despite the harsh nature of our country, it is extremely fragile. The Great Barrier Reef is dying, bushfires have been more devastating than ever, destroying forests untouched for thousands of years. Many of our great and unique species are endangered. This is our responsibility to defend.

I feel that to want to defend Australia, and to serve in its military, is not a matter of wanting to protect our government or its interests, but to protect our mates, our families, this nature, and our way of life. If your military service has ended, and you can no longer serve to defend this country, consider the many ways you could continue your service to protect what we still have.

Beyond just protecting our nature, our service can be continued by taking care of those around us. If we want to care for our country, we can start by taking care of our families. As we are no longer required to go away for long periods of time, we can offer service to those we love and to our community.

Serving Australia doesn't have to be from some great act of courage and sacrifice, it can start with being a good person, by respecting and appreciating what we have, by being a custodian of harmony.

Dreaming

In my heart I have been dreaming
Of a day where we become
A people all in union
In this battle all as one

But this vision's all in tatters
As we're scattered round the coast
By the winds of our ambitions
Far from the ones we love the most

I would give it all up gladly
Just to see that vision clear
Yet my actions lead me further
From the people I hold dear

How could I forsake my own heart
In this search to find the truth
I have lost the very meaning
That I cherished in my youth

In my sleep I will be dreaming
Of those days under the sun
Our family, in freedom
In a battle our hearts won

Dreaming – Reflection

I wrote "Dreaming" to reflect on the feelings of missing those that I love, yet continually being pulled away from them. My family, my mates, my home all call me, yet somehow, I let my mind pull me away from them.

When I was in the Army, this was all part of the job, and I didn't get to choose where I lived. I had to accept that my partner and I would endure years of distance until we finally managed to align my posting with an opportunity for her to live in Australia. Outside of international relationships however, many of our service personnel spend years long distance, classified as a Member with Dependents – Unaccompanied (MWD-U). It's great that we have an acronym for that, emotionally distancing ourselves from what it actually means.

We all find coping strategies for that distance, but quite often this involves putting up walls, as referenced in the following poem "Candle". If we want to grow connections in our hearts, we need to accept the vulnerability that comes with it and express to those we love how much they mean to us, and how much we miss them. It also requires being able to reach out to our families and friends and accepting their help.

I try my best now to express my true feelings to my partner and family, so they can be in my life and connect without barriers. Beyond just my family and partner, I share these feelings with my mates. If I miss them, I tell them. If I am hurting, they will know that too. If I really love them, as important people in my life, I will tell them.

I would love more than anything to have all of the mates I've met over the years, all the great people I've served with, to live in the same place and share in each other's joys and sorrows, but the next best thing is to hold a connection, regardless of distance. The only way to do that is to live with an open heart.

Even now as I am free from the dreaded posting cycle, I haven't moved back home. I have followed the work and the opportunities, and I live with this decision. We all must decide where we will live after our service, and our field of work. If we chose to be apart from those we love, we must remove all the barriers to our hearts to keep those connections strong.

Candle

Our heart is like a candle
That flickers from our speech
Too strong a wind to handle
May extinguish those in reach

Afraid to lose our only light
We hide it deep within
And soon erect the walls to fight
The words that others spin

Alas, the heart is under siege
From more than words outside
Our thoughts begin to plant a seed
To cover what's inside

Soon our walls become a fort
The seed a thorny vine
The candle trapped within is caught
In a prison of the mind

We paint the walls and gates to show
A city of great prestige
When behind this facade we know
Our heart cries to be freed

What others see is what we choose
Our success and personality
Afraid that we might finally lose
Our strength in this identity

This method works when all around
Pretend to be a castle too
Defensiveness and threat abound
At the meeting point of any two

But there are people burning bright
With pure love inside their heart
They shine like stars in the night
And guide the way of where to start

They cover not their brilliant flame
But rather use the walls as fuel
They burn their paintings, palisades and pain
To release their heart from oppressive rule

From a candle to a raging fire
From a fire to a glowing sun
We must burn the falsehoods we acquire
To shine our light and love as one

Candle – Reflection

"Candle" is a metaphor for the two ways in which I have lived my life. Firstly, as a defensive, threatened, insecure person who spent his time building up an identity, an image, walls, status, and so on. Secondly, as someone who is trying to tear down those walls and free my true self. One is false, the other authentic. One is illusion, the other truth.

It can seem easier to live behind walls. We may have an education, position, rank, physical accomplishments, a reputation, work ethic or personality that we hide behind, but the type of wall is irrelevant. It's all a way of hiding the candle, our heart, from being extinguished, but the candle is only vulnerable when the flame is small.

Children play, laugh, sing and dance without a shadow of insecurity until they're judged harshly for it by their parents, teachers or other children who have also had their flame threatened and felt they had to hide it. Once a child learns insecurity, it takes a long time to push past it.

If a child's heart is embraced, however, and allowed to flow into their passion—whether it's music, art, athletics, intelligence, etc.—it's expressed through authentic self-actualisation. Different from building walls to appear strong, this is the genuine expression of someone putting their "whole heart into it".

Many giant fortresses people call an identity, are just convoluted protection mechanisms for childhood shame, humiliation or guilt. Some form of judgement and evaluation hurt them and they launched into the comparison to others that shapes so much of our lives. This ties back to the themes of "Clay" and the haiku, "Childhood Trauma".

Living with an open heart takes great courage, as it is a quick way to draw slings and arrows from others who haven't allowed themselves the same vulnerability. We can still be strong, confident, courageous, and work with a ruthless intensity and yet have an open heart.

It might be unclear what any of this has to do with depression and suicide, but it ties back to the same values. Do we act out of recognition and from a state of lack, or out of contribution, from a state of abundance? Do we hide behind a wall, where our true needs are never met? Or do we live authentically, with more chance of being heard and understood? A great deal of the pain around suicide is connected to our hidden selves.

To grow the candle into a sun, throw all of the layers of self-protection into the fire, expose the light and the dark within, to integrate and heal them. If you're struggling with suicidal depression or anxiety, look for the walls you've built to surround yourself and throw them in the fire.

Practically, what this looked like for me, was to be authentic: honest when I was in pain and honest when I didn't know something or couldn't do it. My walls were perfectionism, so I never confronted the shame of failure or criticism. My walls were my shattered past, which told me opening up would only cause me pain. My walls constantly sought validation and approval from others, so that

I didn't have to bear the weight and consequence of my decisions alone.

Overcoming these walls takes time and practice, but just like the storeroom metaphor, each wall we take down gives us more mental and emotional freedom to gain perspective, grow and heal. Sometimes taking down walls exposes the pain we have hidden beneath. But rather than continue to hide this pain, we must face it. The following poem expresses some of the pain that became apparent to me when I let down my walls.

The later poem "Meditation" provides a tool to help see your heart through these walls and support the process of tearing them down.

Take a moment to consider what walls and mental limitations you may have set up to protect your heart, and how they may be holding you back.

Forgive

I'm a jack sack of shit
That quit because I'm weak
I speak of all these values
But it's shallow what I seek

I ran from all my problems
To solve them, but they repeat
I'm a failure not a saviour
Deserter and a cheat

All this I have tried
To hide the shame inside
Yet it spills from my lungs
While I choke on swallowed pride

There was a moment that I felt
I'd earnt the right to be
A person worth respecting
Reflecting now I see

My ego clear as mud
My deeds of fear and pain
My successes all were dud
My service all in vain

What role model am I?
To the people that I love
When all I do is cry
And fail to rise above

This pain within my mind
Relentlessly unkind
Destroying all I'm worth
One memory at a time

There's no other way to say
The feeling in which I drown
Except in every way
I'm sorry I let you down

Apology accepted
Correct this cold perspective
There's no need to feel rejected
Your pain's to be expected

You're a fucking human being
It's normal to hurt when leaving
And those tears you feel ashamed of
Are perfect for what you're freeing

You're releasing stored emotions
And speaking of fears unspoken
You've awoken something dormant
That needs to be wide open

Those tears come from your heart
It's part of its healing art
You're much stronger by confronting
This darkness so you can start

To forgive yourself for every
Mistake that you have stored
And reward yourself for having
The courage to have explored

All your failures as a chance
To reflect on where to grow
Have the self-compassion now
To embrace what you don't know

You're not running now from shit
Your service was not in vain
So refrain from saying "quit"
When you are still in the game

This is only the beginning
From serving purpose to leaving
Now your service is a journey
To find your new sense of meaning

If you feel that you've let down
Your family or your mates
Your fate's now in your hands
To make all of them proud

So surround yourself with people
That love you for who are
And accept that you have demons
And reasons for all your scars

But begin within yourself
By accepting who's in the mirror
And surrender to this moment
Expose it to see it clearer

That you are not the villain
Or victim within this image
That's a voice within your mind
That's violated your vision

It's a decision you must make
To take back the control
That you are worth forgiveness
Deserving another role

In this story of your life
A role where you can give
Your love to those who matter
Decide now to forgive

Forgive – Reflection

"Forgive" is a poem about feeling that we have failed those we love. We could feel like we have failed our parents, our partners, our mates, or our children. If we feel that we have let them down, we may not give ourselves the space to heal and overcome our own problems. If we truly care about them, the first step is to forgive ourselves so we can begin the process of healing and return to being that person they can rely on.

I placed this poem after "Candle" as the process of tearing down our walls often exposes such hidden pain. Our walls hide these negative self-beliefs that require the most self-compassion to heal.

We often find it easy to forgive others, yet we have this voice in our heads that tears us to pieces. Just as the voice in this poem shifts from self-destructive to empowering, we need to shift the voice in our minds too. This is not easy, but it is possible. We owe it to those we love to be kind to ourselves, so we can offer them the best version of who we are.

The following poem "Meditation" offers a powerful tool to observe the stream of our mind and to find enough presence to forgive ourselves.

Meditation

Take a moment to slow your breathing
And pay attention to your sensations
Feel your stress and tension leaving
Observe with no more expectations

Name five things that you can see
And four more things that you can hear
Now three more things that you can feel
And finally two that you can smell

Let go of these and breathe once more
And plant your feet firm on the floor
One deep inhale down to your core
Exhale, release, repeat, restore

Place one hand upon your chest
And then the other on your pain
Forgive yourself and do your best
To accept what is and try again

Imagine yourself as just a child
That you are now here holding tight
You are its carer and its guide
So give it love and strength to fight

Now in this state of love and kindness
Ask "What am I grateful for?"
There's always something to remind us
Of gifts we can be thankful for

Once we have the power of presence
And see the privilege of our life
We can seek to understand our essence
Our values, purpose and our strife

Life is suffering, the scriptures say
But our greatest purpose can be found
In our obstacles, there is a way
To live with purpose and rebound

Repeat this as a meditation
Read it slow and take each action
You are your own best medication
To clear your mind and regain traction

Meditation – Reflection

"Meditation" is a practical poem to cut through the bullshit. Many people consider meditation an act performed by Zen Buddhists or gurus sitting under trees to attain enlightenment. The truth is we're already here, a single breath away from enlightenment, and there's nothing to attain. It is just the noise of our minds that stops us from seeing what's all around us. As Dan Millman says in his great work *Way of the Peaceful Warrior*, meditation is the sword that cuts through the mind to find clarity.

Imagine if some divine being handed you a certificate that said, "Congratulations! You are now enlightened."

How would your life change?

What would you value?

What would your purpose be?

What would you want from life outside of the military?

What would you want to give to the world?

We may never get rid of the suffering in life, but we can give it meaning.

There is an ancient story about a Zen master seeking enlightenment. After years of searching, he finds an old man carrying a heavy load and immediately upon seeing him, he knows the old man is enlightened. He asks the old man, "What is enlightenment?" and the old man smiled and dropped his pack. Smiling back, the Zen Master said, "Yes, yes, but what comes after enlightenment?" The old man picked up his pack, shouldered the burden, smiled, and continued walking.

There is no fairy tale ending to leaving the military—no happily ever after, just a different burden to shoulder. But if there is anything we can learn from this experience, it's that the burden feels lighter when we carry it with presence, purpose and a sense of privilege.

Ink

From an ink drop come the ten thousand things
A fountain pen with a big bang against the paper
The raw shock of a Rorschach rings
The creator and viewer are one, yet you are stunned

Reaching back to the abyss beyond your form
Where your true self was lost in an eclipse
Hiding your sun behind the moon, you mourn
For the sweet death in your twilight reverie

Patience is a virtue only for those who are waiting
But the virtuous stay present, awaiting nothing
Stationed with a candle, their will creating
They manifest intentions from the heart

The mind knows not this novel method
It convolutes with expectations
This life for suffering to be weathered
Resisting all that is through thought

Observe the ink flow from the tip
It is the only moment that truly exists
The past is consumed with each black drip
The future, only the potential of a pen

Ink – Reflection

"Ink" seeks to capture the passage of time through metaphor. Woven through each line are the various themes from this book along with other references.

The "ten thousand things" alludes to the ancient spiritual text, the *Tao Te Ching*, and the emergence of the entire universe from emptiness. In our case, it is the emergence of our own reality from nothing, created every moment we exist. The "big bang" refers to the creation of the universe, but from the perspective of our self-created reality.

If time is the passing of a pen along a page, the past is what's written, the future is blank paper, and the present is that infinitesimally small point under the tip of the pen—and the only thing that exists. The past is a memory, the future an imagined potential, and only that fleeting point is real.

The "raw shock of a Rorschach rings" refers to the ink blot test, or Rorschach test, once used to understand someone's psyche through their interpretations of otherwise meaningless blobs of ink. In effect, we do the same to our reality. Staring at the tip of the pen from our own subjective perspective, we create our world as much by our actions, as by our belief and bias about what we see. Often by projecting our expectations on the point of the pen, we unconsciously influence the future to unfold in alignment with our thoughts. This is the meaning of the line "the creator and viewer are one".

For example, if we believe that we'll injure ourselves, we might unconsciously project that fear into the present by hesitating or tensing, which can exacerbate or cause injuries. Conversely, if we project optimism when someone asks for help and don't assume they're just using us, we will help them from our heart and reap the true reward of contribution.

In line with the TV metaphor, if we're always focused on what the pen has already written, it will just keep writing the same words repeatedly. If we're truly present, focused on the tip of the pen, believing change is good, suffering and pain are opportunities to grow, and living by values is the way to true meaning, the pen will write far more interesting stories.

In the poem, the "sun" refers to the heart, while the "moon" refers to the subconscious. When our heart, or truest desire, is eclipsed by our mind or impulses, we live in a state of want, rather than from a state of love.

The idea that "the virtuous stay present awaiting nothing" plays on the concept of patience as a virtue and a balance. Those who are patient may spend their lives waiting to live and miss the whole thing. When we live from the heart over the mind, we don't have as much need for patience, as we live each moment for its own sake, not for what the mind stands to gain or lose from it.

The previous poem "Meditation" gives a method to achieve the presence required to see life with open eyes as we allow a new future to be written; one not dictated by the past conditioning mentioned in the poem "Clay".

This poem may seem a stretch from military

transitions, but it's an abstract way of looking at a life that has been written so far in very certain terms before an uncertain future and reflects on how we can embrace change in every moment.

Now you are the one holding the pen. What story will you write?

After Credits

Watch the film with such delight
Immersed in all the brilliant splendour
Cry and laugh or feel the fright
A thirst for all the visions rendered

But light it is reflected back
A screen with speakers that you hear
Perceptions flood your mind in fact
You never really feel the fear

A life we live inside a theatre
Cameras, action, actors, aether
Nothing real to feel or feature
Just illusions one projector

Yet the story all makes sense
God forbid you lose the plot
From start to finish, in sequence
The scenes and acts your mind forgot

But if you are just cause – effect
What of free will and conscious choice
If by a script you do direct
Then sorry, but you have no voice

When the credits roll and pass
And all the players played their part
You wake to find you're in first class
Watching just a work of art

Sitting in the premier screening
What did you do that had meaning?
Did you watch or did you act?
Did you play or just react?

Now the credits have all gone
And you are not inside the screen
You are the witness and the pawn
You are the actor and the scene

For we are all the roles in one
Director, actor, set, observer
We are the world and the sun
The universe and its fervour

Ourselves we limit by this logic
That all the scenes have to connect
A journey do we think, it's tragic
Our heart has no chance to reflect

If you want to have free will
Then see it all as just a dance
Forget a path that keeps you still
And live as such to take each chance

To dance is never to arrive
Or set a goal to feel alive
It is to move and live each breath
Regardless where you end at death

Thankfully there is still time
You haven't quite missed out just yet
The after-credits are sublime
For they are free and never set

If you could live beyond the story
Without the rules of who you are
Of how to live or want for glory
Where would you choose to set your star?

Make it bloopers, or a teaser
Make it super or a breezer
Flip the script on who you are
And follow with an open heart

After Credits – Reflection

"After Credits" asks us to discard the self-imposed limitations of our past and our identity. We do not need to forget our past or pretend it never happened, but we can still choose to be whoever we want in this life and don't need to trap ourselves by what's behind us. We are the creators of our own world. We have the capacity to change our reality for the better.

Our conscious experiences and perceptions of the world are just electrical impulses in our brains, much like the sights and sounds from a movie projector. We project our beliefs of the world onto what we see, until it makes sense, and if our beliefs are shaped by our past, we'll only ever see the same patterns repeat in our lives. To be truly free, we must see the present moment with clarity, as it is, not how we believe it to be.

Clarity is rare, as our self-deception is so clever, it's almost invisible. We can deceive ourselves of what we can and can't do all our lives.

Finding stillness can show us that the ways we've defined ourselves in the past were illusions, only projections of our past. Through clarity, we can continue to see who we are, without all the layers and facades, and we can see it's ever changing.

We may not know what we want. We do not know how our lives will go. We do not have control over much at all. We can only know the present moment, and we can only control how we choose to perceive it and what values we choose to stand for. Yet through these small slivers of freedom, we can create our own world.

Closing Remarks

We each experience our journeys differently and not everyone will struggle with the more intense emotional aspects of transitioning from Defence. The rate of suicide and depression among our veteran community tells me that I'm not alone in finding it difficult, and if you've struggled, you're not alone either.

These poems tell a story. All service must end. We all must find the balance of belonging and maintaining our freedom. If we have served, we're all veterans, no matter the length of service. The process of leaving the military involves a letting go, an acceptance, and the work to actively untangle the knots and eventually reconnect.

As we transition into civilian life, we must find what we value and uncover the purpose we choose to live for. Finally, we must find ways not just to cope with the struggle, but to become stronger through it, to be fuelled by it, and to grow.

This is by no means the complete solution to address our problems during and after service, but it's a start. It's a call to arms to share our stories, to ask for help, and to offer it.

I hope that through this short volume of poetry, you found something worth taking away into your life—whether it is a new perspective, the desire to find your values, to meditate, or to read. More than anything, I hope it helps you overcome whatever you are struggling with, so you too can share your lessons and reach out to someone else in a time of need.

Acknowledgements

I have many people to thank to still be here to write this to you, too many to put into this acknowledgement.

The greatest pillar in my life has been my partner, Marta. She has shown strength and courage that surpasses anything I saw in my service, but more importantly she showed me the deepest of love, which allowed for all my turmoil and turbulence to be calmed and overcome. Her understanding and patience have given me the space to unpack all of what I write in this book, and the courage to be able to share it. I owe her my life.

To all my mates, who have been there to listen, to talk, to understand, and at times, to give me the right amount of banter to pick me up. Thank you.

To all those I had the privilege to serve alongside, thank you for your dedication, hard work, and your contribution. Though it was my job to lead my soldiers, I gained far more inspiration from them, and was often in awe at their creativity, ingenuity, skill, and passion.

Finally, to you, whoever you are, thank you for reading this book. If it helps you even in the slightest way, it has made this journey worthwhile.

References

The following are resources and references that gave me support and inspired the poetry in this book.

Books

The following books are displayed in order of recommendation to read:

The Reality Slap by Dr Russ Harris
The Courage to be Disliked by Ichiro Kishimi and Fumitake Koga
Explain Pain by David Butler and Lorimer Moseley
Lost Connections by Johann Hari
Tribe by Sebastian Junger
The Biology of Belief by Dr Bruce Lipton
The Power of Vulnerability by Brené Brown
Man's Search for Meaning by Viktor Frankl
Extreme Ownership by Leif Babin and Jocko Willink
Way of the Peaceful Warrior by Dan Millman
The Power of Now by Eckhart Tolle
The Body Keeps the Score by Bessel van der Kolk
The Power of Habit by Charles Duhigg

Resources

Brothers n Books
https://www.facebook.com/BrothersNBooks
What? Me worry?
https://www.cci.health.wa.gov.au/Resources/Looking-After-Yourself/Worry-and-Rumination
42for42
https://www.42for42.org.au/
Mates4Mates
https://mates4mates.org/
Solider On
https://soldieron.org.au/

Phone Numbers

Open Arms 1800 011 046
Lifeline 13 11 14
Mates4Mates 1300 462 837